*Thy word is a lamp unto my feet,
and a light unto my path*

Psalm 119:105

The Spiritual Quest

An Adventure With God

The Spiritual Quest by Max Stitts

Copyright © 2004 by Maxel L. Stitts
All Right Reserved

ISBN: 0-9754332-3-7

Published by: **Advantage Books**
www.advbooks.com

This book and parts thereof may not be reproduced in any form, stored in a retrieval system or transmitted in any form by any means (electronic, mechanical, photocopy, recording or otherwise) without prior written permission of the author, except as provided by United States of America copyright law.

Library of Congress Control Number: 2004110185

Cover Design by: Pat Theriault
Photo of Max Stitts by: Patty Foppen

First Printing: October 2004

04 05 06 07 08 09 10   7 6 5 4 3 2 1

Printed in the United States of America

Acknowledgments

I have been blessed by my wife Velma for forty-nine years, and her faithfulness to the Lord Jesus is a living testimony. Our three children love the Lord, and my heart is warmed when I speak their names – Mark, Mike, and Sheryl.

God has his hand on and his voice in *The Spiritual Quest*. This book would not have made it into public hands without his guidance. Likewise, this publication would not have been possible without the help of many dear friends. Their spirits and devotion to the Lord have been a constant encouragement and blessing to me.

I have read in many books where people's names were given, and they were thanked for their help. I want to go beyond words and ask the Lord to give a spiritual blessing to Mark and Barb Yoder. They have shown a spiritual dedication not only to the work of *The Spiritual Quest*, but they have blessed everyone around them as they faithfully serve the Lord Jesus.

Brent and Esther Hochstetler, like the Yoders, have given of themselves tirelessly with typing and editing. Their love for the Lord shines like a beacon light, and I ask the Lord to give them a special blessing as well.

I would like to thank Alfred and Jody Ebersol for both their spiritual and financial support. May the Lord bless them abundantly for their help in this endeavor.

Additionally, I would like to thank Donna Rode. She willingly gave of her time to help finalize the editing at the very last minute. I lift up a blessing for her as well.

And, of course, I thank God for the blessings he has given me throughout my life. To this end, I have had, for many years, a brass business cardholder on which the three letters *G.F.B.* are engraved. People say to me, "Your name is Max Stitts. What does the G.F.B. stand for?" My reply has always been, "This cardholder has been engraved with G.F.B. to remind me of the correct order for my life. The *G* stands for God, and he is first. The *F* stands for family, and they are second. The *B* stands for business, and it is always last, behind God and family."

CONTENTS

The Quest Begins 9

SERIES I

Lesson 1	The Spiritual Quest	17
Lesson 2	The Presence of God	21
Lesson 3	God's Splendor	25
Lesson 4	Spiritual Patience...	29
Lesson 5	Spiritual Nourishment	33
Lesson 6	Life and Death: Physical Illusion and Spiritual Reality.................................	37
Lesson 7	The New Life	51

SERIES II

Lesson 8	The Kingdom Within	61
Lesson 9	Sonship in His Spirit..	65
Lesson 10	Spiritual Truth	69
Lesson 11	Spiritual Refreshment	73
Lesson 12	Spiritual Light	79
Lesson 13	This Age's Wisdom	81
Lesson 14	All Knowing	87

SERIES III

Lesson 15	Old Treasures in New Canvas	93
Lesson 16	The Service of the Scribe	99
Lesson 17	Spiritual Humility in Royal Robe	105
Lesson 18	The Nature of God	109
Lesson 19	God's Healing Love	113
Lesson 20	Spiritual Blessings and Peace	117
Lesson 21	The Center of Man	123

SERIES IV

Lesson 22	The Inward Journey	129
Lesson 23	The Outward Journey	135
Lesson 24	The Earthly Man Becomes the Spiritual Son	141
Lesson 25	To Know Even As You Are Known	145
Lesson 26	Striving After God	149
Lesson 27	Overflowing Joy	155
Lesson 28	Spiritual Asking of the Lord	161

SERIES V

Lesson 29	Spiritual Questions	169
Lesson 30	Spiritual Joy	173
Lesson 31	Spiritual Prosperity	177
Lesson 32	The Displeasure of God	181
Lesson 33	The Matter of Truth	185
Lesson 34	World Peace	189
Lesson 35	God's Power	193

SERIES VI

Lesson 36	Deeper Meanings of Life	199
Lesson 37	Love's Deeper Meaning	203
Lesson 38	Spiritual unto Physical Manifestation	207
Lesson 39	The True Meanings of Abundance	211
Lesson 40	Sensing: Physical and Spiritual	217
Lesson 41	Spiritual Creativity	223
Lesson 42	Spiritual Growing	229

SERIES VII

Lesson 43	Spiritual Instruction	235
Lesson 44	Light and Darkness: Shades of the Spirit ...	239
Lesson 45	Physical and Spiritual Sin	243
Lesson 46	The Spiritual Offering / Heavenly Cautions	249
Lesson 47	Values, Both Earthly and Spiritual	253
Lesson 48	The Glory of the True New Age	257
Lesson 49	The Future from this Day Forth	263

THE QUEST BEGINS

Back in the early 1970s, my family and I built a lodge we called home in the mountains of Kentucky. During a season of prayer and meditation, it became clear to me the Lord was speaking to my spirit. At first, I reacted with "This can't be real," and "Am I putting these words into my own head?" Finally, I yielded my spirit to God's Spirit, and the lessons began.

Over a period of many days, the lessons came. I listened with spirit ears and wrote down what I heard. That is why I cannot claim to be the author of *The Spiritual Quest*, only the scribe.

My family was in Lexington, Kentucky, and I was speaking at a local hotel when I received the message that our lodge in the mountains had been struck by lightning and had burned to the ground. Everything we owned in the lodge, including *The Spiritual Quest*, was gone.

Over twenty years passed, and I thought that the lessons were gone forever. I was truly blessed by having *The Spiritual Quest* if only for a brief period of time.

Then one day, I received a call from a friend in Denver, Colorado. He said he was moving some boxes around in his attic and found some writings I had sent him many years ago. He read the first page of the first lesson, and I knew immediately what it was. I had mailed him a copy of *The Spiritual Quest* and had forgotten that he had a copy. It was quite clear that God had plans for *The Spiritual Quest* beyond my personal edification and blessing.

I shared the lessons with some dear friends who responded as I did. They told me how God had blessed them as they read *The Spiritual Quest*. With their encouragement and support, along with several others, *The Spiritual Quest* is published with the prayer that spirit-directed, God-seeking people will be blessed as we have been.

Some of the things foretold in these lessons have already come to pass while still others are in our future.

On more of a personal note, some of my friends have encouraged me to share what might be called the story within the story of the forty-nine lessons called *The Spiritual Quest*.

Late one night after my wife and children had gone to bed, I was up reading and praying and asking God a lot of questions. Suddenly, an answer to one of my questions was voiced in my head. Then all kinds of thoughts raced through my head, thoughts like, "Did I just answer my own question?", "Where did that voice come from?", and "What is going on here?" I then prayed, "Lord, I do not want to think up answers and say I got them from you."

I backed off and told no one, and for about seven to ten days, everything was silent. Then again late one night, that same voice spoke and said, "Can we just talk?" I can tell you I did very little talking and a lot of listening. It seemed like it lasted only a few minutes, but the night was gone, and I saw the sunrise in the east. Still, I suppose I was not ready to accept what was going on.

This time, several more weeks passed, and I remained silent about the experience. The third time, the voice said, "Would you take a pen and write?"

I replied, "Yes," and then asked, "What am I to write?"

The voice said, "I call these *Letters from Home*."

So I began, as a scribe, writing *Letters from Home*. The letters dealt with personal issues and things going on in the community where I lived. With each letter, I was becoming more relaxed and less fearful that I was creating things in my head. Over and over again, I prayed to the Lord that if he was not in the things I was writing down, please stop the letters and clear up my head. You may think it was foolish on my part not to be able to recognize the voice of the Lord, but back in the early 1970s, I didn't know of anyone saying God spoke to them. Today, all over the world, God's children are hearing from him and allowing the Holy Spirit to direct their lives, but back when my experience began, it was not well received. I just kept all of the letters to myself and thanked the Lord for the special blessings. I would love to share some of the letters, but when our home burned to the ground, all of the letters were lost. The letters were gone, but my blessings remained.

Finally, I suppose, I reached a comfort level or a spiritual condition where the Lord could get to a deeper matter. He spoke and told me we were to deal with a series of lessons. There would be seven lessons in each series and seven series in total. I was instructed to call the series *The Spiritual Quest*.

At this point, I was willing to get a pen and paper, get off by myself, and listen and write, and keep self out of the way. I was allowed to ask questions. Sometimes I wrote them down (my questions and comments are in italics) and other times, because I was so excited to hear the answers, I did not write them down. As a result, there are some instances where the flow of the letters may appear to change or jump around slightly.

Besides this book, the Lord provided me with another series of lessons called *The Willow for the World*. This series describing seven branches of human needs will be published at a later time.

By the time *The Spiritual Quest* is published, I will have experienced my seventy-fifth birthday. I do not know how many more years I have, but I can say, without question, I know who I will be serving: As for me and my house, we will serve the Lord.

I am not called to defend *The Spiritual Quest*, only to say to let the Holy Spirit direct you and to read this book with your spirit eyes. That God may speak to your spirit as he has mine and that he may lift you to a more committed walk with him are my prayers for you. It has been nearly thirty years now since the Lord first spoke to my spirit. *The Spiritual Quest* has been held in God's keeping until now.

God brought the Yoders and the Hochstetlers and others into our lives, giving encouragement and support. It is under God's directive that I share these forty-nine spiritual lessons with you. I pray they encourage you in spirit to draw more closely to your heavenly Father.

God's timing is always perfect, and the time has come for these lessons to be shared with you and the world.

Be blessed in his name,

Scribe Maxie

The Spiritual Quest

The Spiritual Quest

Series One

I

The Spiritual Quest

LESSON 1

THE SPIRITUAL QUEST

Let us speak of the spiritual quest. Men will ask of me many questions, all of which I am most willing to answer, but as soon as they ask, for the most part they go on about other matters not willing to know I am ready to answer even before they ask me. There are others who lift their faces skyward crying out for answers, and they are filled with desire to know, but look in the wrong places for the answers they seek.

These lessons are prepared for man so he may be able, in the true spirit, to have all that he seeks and, then, even a measure to make him overflow.

I have clearly said to man, "Seek ye first the kingdom, and I will add all other things to fill your fondest spiritual dreams."

Because man is so physically oriented, for the most part he relates his searching to the physical. He asks for signs and looks at the clouds or the bending of the pine tree and makes of them answers of his own choosing.

I am not saying there are not answers in the physical realm where man's form dwells, but I am making it clear that spirit answers in the spirit, and then at the very last, the form may see what has already been made clear to the spirit.

You ask, "How is it then that nature will give forth her signs?" Have I not said that man has dominion over all things of the world? So man still rules the earthly things for they are subject to man. The turmoil and chaos of the physical are all of man's doing.

Did not my Son the Christ calm the waves of the sea that had caused fear to enter the hearts of the men around him?

He did not seek to do battle with the storm as a man would stand. He but called upon the spirit within, for we are of one spirit, and as the true Son, he calmed the sea before the very eyes of his followers.

He did not use a power that was available only unto himself and not to the followers who were with him. He but used what I have given every man.

Peter, like Christ, walked upon the water. Are you and Peter different forms of men, or would you say to me, "We are the same man"? Then let me direct the spirit of man so that he will once again rule with his spirit and not with his form.

Do you not see that everything you now have would have been a miracle to the ancient kings? You could have been head of the court of wise men in most kingdoms with a match in the center of your palm. "Miracles!" men would say. "No," you would cry, "it is only a match. They are of

The Spiritual Quest

little value and nearly no cost." "Miracle all the more!" they would cry.

The spiritual quest of these lessons is to bring men to the knowing of matters of the spirit so they may ask in the spirit and have their answers even while asking.

It is important now for man to be taught these lessons for he is on a course that will destroy the garden of my making. If he refuses – and the destruction will surely come if he does – then all who are knowing will be full in the spirit, and for them there can be no loss. When the energy of the form is destroyed, it but returns unto the source whence it came.

Say unto all men, "That which is spiritual is eternal, and the very fires of hell cannot give off enough heat to make itself known to the true spirit. That which is of the earthly form is naught but a manifestation and does not even have existence in relation to the eternal." This first series has begun; let these words speak unto the spirit of man.

If one says they are not for me, know that the form is speaking, not the spirit, and no truer words could come forth from his mouth.

It is but the first step of seven that we are to take together. Rest in my Spirit, and you will be cradled in eternal love.

The Spiritual Quest

LESSON 2

THE PRESENCE OF GOD

I would speak to you now of the presence of God.

Man spends many idle seasons on his knees in prayer when his spirit is far from me. Would it not be better for his spirit to kneel before me in the presence of my Spirit? For then we are truly together, and all that the spirit of man seeks, the spirit receives.

The form of the earthly cannot come into my presence for I am spirit. Man has placed his sense of values wrongly. Worship me in spirit and in truth, not in body and mind. After your spirit is in my presence, then the form, which you call the body, of that spirit will do exactly as it is directed by man's spirit, and it shall be as I would have it, for then we are one and of the same spirit.

Do you not see? The error is not in getting on your knees to praise me, or to stand and to sing praises to my name and to lift high your hands in supplication. It is but the order of your doing that you must change.

When the child drinks his milk, he is not always ready for the meat which is to follow. I would that you would be nourished upon both.

The praise of the form with the absence of the spirit is what I have called the "waste of idle time."

Stand in my presence with your spirit, and see then how the form will praise me with a new exaltation.

Speak from the form of man when your spirit is in my presence, and the words will ring like the thunder of the early spring storm.

Clap your hands and lift your voices, for you will then be joined by angelic choirs.

Let your spirit be in me, for that is the meaning of our spirits in oneness, and you will see and hear the songs of my choosing and the words of my mouth. Then you will know what it is I have planned for my spiritual church. I do not speak of the physical form for it is but a manifestation of the real and is as temporal as the cutting of the fall grass that burns to light the ovens of man.

Do you now see clearly that man is still preoccupied with the form and has not yet gone to the source?

Which burns the hotter, the coal that man digs from the earth (for coal is but form) or the energy that is the source for the form you dig?

Man has not yet begun to use what I have planned for him. He has been too preoccupied with the mirrored image to come to the real where he will find me.

This lesson is finished. But oh how few there are who have learned fully of it!

The amount of my filling is dependent upon the size of the container offered unto me to be filled.

The Spiritual Quest

LESSON 3

GOD'S SPLENDOR

Would you have another lesson now?

Would you give now?

You have but to open, for my giving is ever flowing. See even now how you closed the floodgate for a moment and nothing came through. So do you not see that it is man that shuts out the flow, not the Father, for my flow is like the ever-moving river of life? You may go to it and bathe at will, and you will be washed as clean as my Spirit.

Know you all this day that the gate of my splendor is seen when you are not so busy looking with your eyes so you may behold the splendor without burning you into blindness.

If you would look at your sun for any moment beyond your simple sensing, you would see naught but the sun and find the tree in your path. My splendor is as a thousand suns, each a thousand times more brilliant than the one before, and each adds its brilliance to the one before it.

Would you ask to see it? Or would it be better to ask to be it? For in being, you share the splendor, and then it is not too much for your viewing. If you would see me, you must first become part of what it is you wish to view.

Man has said, "Where can I find God?" and I say, "Look within man."

Would you search for me with human hands and seek to touch the sun?

Did not my son and servant Moses seek to see me in the burning bush? It was but a dim reflection of his look inward, and then but a ray of light was too much for his people to behold.

Light does not fade. You say it faded from the face of Moses, but I say unto you the gate was closed that allowed my splendor to break through. It did not fade; it was lessened only by my servant of his own choosing. He found a power that he feared for his people.

You have found it – the door of my splendor! Do you fear to open it?

No.

Then its use must be good, or it will first destroy the user. This was to Moses's knowing as well.

I would not have my splendor splashed like cold water into the faces of my children. It is light to be given to my children who seek the light.

This lesson has all within it. The order of the learning is with you. For when the order of using is correct, the light of my gate of splendor will be seen by your being. Thus saith the Lord.

God's Splendor

And this lesson is finished, as is the one before it.

Rest, for the night is over and already the rays of a simple sun are preparing to step upon the stage of your presence. Thus saith the Lord.

The Spiritual Quest

LESSON 4

SPIRITUAL PATIENCE

Write, and if men heed my words, soon we will have scribes the world over helping their brothers and sisters around them. I have been preparing many who have been looking and waiting for the signs from my Spirit to call unto their spirits.

Wait upon me, and I will direct thy paths. This is an important lesson for all men. Would it not be better for men to do in a moment what they may take years to discover? Then which would be of more value, to allow me to direct his path – even if there be days pass when seemingly nothing is being done – or to compound his errors daily with much activity?

The sheep have learned from the shepherd to wait until he leads them. They may be assured of green pastures when their waiting is over.

It may seem to you that nothing is being done when man learns to be patient and wait upon me, but much is going on that may not be apparent to his sensing. There is an energy vibration of man that puts every organ of his body – my temple – in harmony each with the other. When that harmony is reached, there are many other changes that are apparent to the narrow range of man's sensing. Many forms of sickness, both of mind and body, are unable to penetrate the protective shield of the form that vibrates in harmony with itself. For then it can find a higher harmony of the spirit.

Let it be clearly understood that the true, the ideal, the spirit of man always is in harmony, and thus, it holds the form of that spirit together. Patience is one of the keys to get the body in harmony with itself, and then it can easily become one with the spirit that holds it even now. When these two have become one, can you not see that our spirits can then become one? The temple of my building will once again be ready for the many treasures that are my joy to place within it.

As you read this lesson, sit where you are and wait for me, for I am as close as your inbreathing.

You will find the greatest activity occurs when the form is still. For then the spirit, which maintains its existence by this harmonious power of which I speak, can actively do its much-needed work upon the form that it wishes to assist in every way.

Observe the cricket when it is in a container not of its choosing. If you extend your hand to lift it to safety, it will all the more spring from one place to another trying to avoid the very assistance it was seeking but moments before.

To me, you are like the cricket, for I would lift you up to the safety you seek and set you on a path of great joy and success, but the more I reach to assist you, the more frantic becomes your leaping. Finally, without energy and with much damage to the form, your leaping is ended, but when you are lifted up, you have little energy of movement left to enjoy your new place of grandeur.

Movement is the loss of energy; great movement is the loss of great energy.

When the form is silent without movement and without thought, it is then ready to be lifted up and set upon the path of my choosing. As I have said, "The shepherd leads his flock to the safety and greenery of the valley of love and quiet." Would I not do even more for my sons and daughters?

O God! Thank you for your truth that sets me free!

When I set man free, he is free indeed.

Rest now and take refreshment.

The Spiritual Quest

Spiritual Nourishment

LESSON 5

SPIRITUAL NOURISHMENT

Take the pen in hand and write as I speak.

There has been good growth in the seeds which I have planted. Can you now know of what I speak even as you write these words? The oneness that I have spoken of will come. For the tree of my planting is beside the flow of living water, and you will never thirst. When the tree is fully grown, it will bear much fruit of many varieties.

"Many varieties," you ask, "from one tree?"

It is a tree of many branches, and each branch shall have its own kind of fruit to bear. This is a tree of my planting and not of your own.

Nourish the tree with true praise, not that men may hear, but so I may hear and you may know.

Nourish the tree by the being of my Word. Is it not true that my Word is life and truth and gives man true purpose and being? Then my Word is nourishment. You may read it as I spoke to the prophets of old, or you may speak it now for am I not using you as a prophet this day.

There is no age to my truth. Have I not said it is old treasures in new canvas? Am I not able to talk to men today who will hearken unto the words of my mouth?

Even now, do you feel the joy leaping within you? That is nourishment for the seed that has been planted within you.

I would speak to the millions of the world and of this nation that my truth shall set them free and that they shall be free indeed.

We can have joy to overflowing in all nations when men will once again walk in newness of my Spirit. Is not your walk nourishment to the seed within you? My Spirit's seed of me, when planted, will also nourish daily.

Do you now see that the growth is dependent upon you? You must give for the seed to grow. It is dependent upon me for my Spirit will balance your nourishment with that of my own nourishment. You may grow at a natural rate with natural nourishment. Or you may excel. For with all that you give, I will balance by the nourishment of my Spirit.

Thus saith the Lord, "This is a lesson for all men to learn: For as they give, so will they receive."

Can you outgive the only true and faithful Giver of all there is to give?

You are like the child at the passing of the plate of love-giving. "Give to me, Father, that I may place in the plate my love to you," are the words of a child. So would I not give in abundance to the one who loves me with an abundance?

My giving is not dependent upon your loving. However, is not your loving dependent upon my giving? For I am love!

O Lord, take me up for I am in the joy of your presence.

Speak now my name, for I am your God. And when you speak it in the spirit, it is my very name that has the power to lift you as you have requested. If you would come unto me now, you have but to speak my name: *God.*

O Father God, I love you. I love you, and you are love.

So we are one and lifted up.

Know that the Creator has used this hand today.

O God, Father God, use all of me.

For what is spirit but all? For the next four days, you will receive each day a lesson.

There will be seven in this first series, and there will be seven series; each will be like unto a step. Remember as a child you spoke of seven steps up, and it was written by you at age thirteen.

I would have used you then, but…I need not say more. You will call these lessons *The Spiritual Quest.*

Yes, in answer to your question, there will be forty-nine lessons.

Is there more to follow after the forty-nine?

Why ask of that when you only have a few of the forty-nine with many to follow?

LESSON 6

LIFE AND DEATH: PHYSICAL ILLUSION AND SPIRITUAL REALITY

Part 1

Why are some children born perfect and others born imperfect?

Why are some born in love and others are not loved? Why are some children beaten and starved nearly to death? Why do these difficult things happen to children? The children have not rejected you.

Write.

The suffering you feel as you ask the question is mine as well. I made for man a place where all was to be good. It is the way I have made it for men.

The seed of man can bring forth no more than the fullness that the seed has within.

Man in his rebellion has made the changes that you speak of. They are not mine. I have made the law of love, and my love for every man is as it has always been. I am spirit, and these are the acts of a man who has turned his spirit from me.

The beating of the child is the frustration of the parent visited upon the child.

All were to be born in love, for all men were made in love, and they give forth that which lies deep within. The man's being is what he is able to share! Man's outward action is a reflection of his inner self.

When will it all end?

When man once again loves, he will give forth love to his children, and it will be as it had never been for the child is quick to forgive. The child, so harshly treated, has the ability to respond without holding the adult accountable. "I hold the adult accountable," saith the Lord thy God, "until the true return unto the spiritual."

Lift up your knowing, and you have helped lift the knowing of all men.

Father, someone close to me asks, "Is that which is visited upon the child justice for a previous act? Is the child here once again?"

I ask you to rest now so you may be clear when I speak, for I will answer the question in truth for it has come to me in that same spirit of truth.

Lord, please keep me aside so your truth may come forth.

There is much that I speak in truth that is beyond the mind of knowing man. Truth is, by its nature, unbending to accommodate the

Life and Death: Physical Illusion and Spiritual Reality

shortcomings of man. I speak in terms of the spirit, and the mind of man cannot arrive at a place of clear understanding of my words.

When I speak, you must grow up to meet this truth face to face.

Write.

Thus saith the Lord, "The true life of man never ends." I speak of the spiritual, not the physical. It was my intention that man not taste of death, and so I have clearly stated. One day, man will have the final victory over death. He will then be in the place of my true splendor.

The life of the tree is extended by its seed, and thus, it moves from life unto life, cycle by cycle. The tree knows of me in its life-to-life cycle and in the period of rest between its seasons of fall and spring. Spring gives it new life till the next spring. It had no season of death, only rest. This is as I had planned it for man. His spirit never dies; his physical was to move from spring to its summer and fall, then to its season of rest, and then on to its new spring once again.

Sin in the earthly man injected a new course for the rest season of earthly man's being. He now moved from spring to summer, to fall, to death. This was the cycle of the temporal man, while the same being in his spiritual reality moved only to a time of rest.

Man was born; he grew, became mature, and was to be of full service. When his season of rest came, he would take his earthly form away for a season. I will describe this in detail later.

As you look at the tree in the winter, it only appears to be dead; there is much life within. So it was intended for man, and when he was ready, he could take his form to a new place of responsibility and allow his seed to follow after him, not only children of his physical being, but also children of his spiritual raising. Thus, in my original plan, man on this earth was placed here to glorify the Father of his making. It was all good, and man would have finished his work here on your earth plane and gone on to greater works.

Now you know it was never my intention for man to have to go through the stages he now has to in order to get to life unto life.

Know that on the spiritual plane where your true being dwells, there has been no change, so the real being goes from life to maturity, to rest, to more life. There is no death!

If that is the truth – which it is – can you not see the great illusion created by man called death?

Rest is not death. Death is an act of the physical man because of his sin; it has no reality to it. That which is real has permanence. Death is not permanent; therefore, it is not real.

Man lays the life down only to have to return and pick it up and carry it on a little further. This is, like death, an illusion. It is called by some men "real"; it is given the term *reincarnation*. It has no reality to it at all. That which is God-made is real; that which is man-made is not real.

I have not said that it is this way in the real, only in the illusionary, or the unreal, world in which you live.

You, the spirit man, asks me, "Is there a reincarnation in man?"

I am spirit, as are you, and I say, "Never." There can be no reincarnation

Life and Death: Physical Illusion and Spiritual Reality

in a being that has never died.

You, the shadow of the real man, asks me, "Is there a reincarnation in man?"

For the man of the flesh who has given control to the temporal, the temporal says, "Yes, it is of your making, the same as you created death."

They are both illusions. They are not real. They are not eternal.

You, the spirit man, can make it as one journey in me that never ends, but goes from maturity to rest, to maturity. All is life, even the season of rest.

You, the shadow of the real man, can follow your own way of folly. You say you can be born, then mature, grow and learn, and move forward in your spiritual knowing.

You also say you then lay your life down in rest – "die" as you put it – only to have to return as a child of my love. Again you grow to your maturity, learn of my spiritual calling, move forward, and then lay your life down, or die as you put it.

I say spiritual knowing cannot be held in part; you must return unto me. In your illusion, in each return you will have with you all that you were or are. Remember, it is only an illusion of your own making. You have made the journey harder and longer for yourself. It is not of my making.

Men ask me why don't I do something. I did! I sent my Son the Christ to bring as many as would follow him. A few did, but as the years passed, you have taken his words – most of which were never kept – and made them fit your own illusion.

He said, "You shall never die." He also said, "Though he were dead, yet shall he live." You have made that into new meanings so you can continue your illusion and die now, backed by the Word of God. My Word is life, and there is no death in me or my words at all. Give up now the teachings of man, and let me speak to you, for you are spirit of my Spirit and life of my life, and in you there is no death at all. Thus saith the Lord thy God.

You asked me, "Why does one child come into the home of love while another is beaten and killed with no love at all?" I ask you, "Why is it man is so determined to die at all? Why does he inflict such upon the innocent child?" It is an energy within himself that will run its course to its very end, for there he will have nothing to destroy and, finally, will even have no purpose in his dying. Then he will be either at the pause of or at the end of his rebellion, and he will find I am there waiting with the offer of life. Even the illusion will run to the end and have nothing left to allude to.

Have I not said man can run to the far ends of the earth and he will find me there waiting?

Can you now see that when I made man free to choose, it is my law of love in action again? Go to the end of your rebellion, and I will be there.

Now for the child who is the object of this rebellion. Children are young like a new seed that sprouts out of the ground. Once born, all that they are is full in their knowing. They are not limited, there is no death, they are mine, and I take them unto myself.

Life and Death: Physical Illusion and Spiritual Reality

To die as a child is not to die at all. For that one, the illusion is over, and he is with me to grow and to mature and to prepare for the true period of rest. If in his mind's knowing he thinks he must return to live only to die again, he returns. He returns to the illusion of earthly life while the true spiritual life continues from childhood to adulthood, to rest, to adulthood for new labors in my Spirit.

I have spoken, and there are still truths to be shared. The limitation is with you, and when you are ready, we will deal with this matter further.

Some will read these words and cry out unto me, "He lies." He has not lied; he has not spoken at all. I have said it, and it is the truth. Stand against it with all your strength, and see when you are finished how weak you are.

To my scribe, I say do not defend or exhort on this matter; it will stand alone as it has these ages past.

I have written this so that you will give up the illusion now. Then you will find there is no death, reincarnation, pain, suffering, and all the rest of your mirrored darkness you call light reflection. There is no light in them at all. I am light, and I am not in these things I have spoken of.

"It is finished!' thus saith the Lord thy God.

Men ask me, "Why are some children born limited? Why must they suffer?"

Write so that you may know, and knowing, you may be able to share.

The child born blind has no knowing of a limitation, and so for that one, there is no limitation. There is a far greater limitation that you have when you have all your senses, which man calls full sensing. I say you are greatly limited, and to my knowing, there is sadness. You do not have a knowing of this truth.

Let me speak of pain and suffering.

They come later into the consciousness of man, and then once there, the pain and suffering are great.

For the infant, his knowing of pain and suffering are very little, but his crying, which is his level of knowing, is great. The child cries a great deal and is heard often, but his pain, as an adult knows of it, is not there. Have I not said I will give nothing that you are not able to bear? Would I give a child who is helpless and defenseless the responsibility to carry what is not yet for his knowing?

The infant knows only infant pain in suffering, which is to an adult no pain or suffering at all. Do not in your adult mind then impose on the child a level of suffering and pain that is not his? He may cry much, but the level of suffering is no greater for him where he is than yours is for you.

You often think that at birth there is great suffering for the mother. I say the suffering is known by the child being born as well. His security and life structure have been changed since the life before birth is in no way like the life after birth.

The child knows his own kind of anxiety. It is not more than he can stand. It is, nonetheless, there to his limited knowing.

The damaged child does not know, and to him, there is no state of damage at all.

When man looks upon another, he does not look at what is there; he looks at what he sees to be there and then draws false conclusions based on a false set of facts from the beginning.

To the child of much crying, there is little suffering and pain. That is how it is and how I have always made it to be. To the adult looking on with much more knowing, there is more pain and suffering in his mind than in the mind and body of the child.

Observe the lamb as she brings forth her young. She will not sound forth as the kid is born. She will chew her food as if her birth and her meal are normally at the same time of her natural bringing forth. So it was first with man. Have I not said that before man ate the fruit of knowing and knowing not, there was no pain for he did not know there was an existence of pain? Woman knew, and then the pain was as to her knowing.

Can you now see? Seeing, take heart and love and live in me without pain and suffering and all of these man-made limitations.

Part 2

The words that I have spoken unto you in this lesson are not to be changed. Would I tell you one thing of truth, only to later tell you it was not truth at all?

Also know this: The order of the lessons has not been given to you.

When the forty-nine lessons are finished, I will then give you the proper order for each of the seven series and for the seven lessons which are to go in each of these series.

This lesson was given to you, and I asked you to write what I spoke without making any change. It is even now to remain without change. We will now give you a clear understanding of each of my expressions.

"We will now give?"

Yes, we. Am I not father-mother God? Are not Christ and I one? Is not the spirit a part of that same oneness? Are you not part of the same "we"?

Yes, I am.

Let us go on.

I have made it very clear there is much beyond the mind-knowing of man. I am spirit and I speak in spirit, so do not try to find the answers by using your mind in the searching.

When people say we do not understand the words in a lesson, tell them they examined the words with their minds and not with their spirits. "The problem is with them and not with my words," saith the Lord God.

Did I not tell you at the end of a lesson, there would be rejection of my words? It should not concern you. In fact, theirs is not a rejection, only the wrong use of their tools.

I said, "You must grow up to meet this truth face to face." The growth I spoke of is spiritual, and only when man turns will he be face to face

Life and Death: Physical Illusion and Spiritual Reality

with me, for I am truth.

The true life never ends. I am spirit, and it is the spirit life I speak of. I did not intend for the physical man to die. The physical was to be under the control of the spirit, so it was my plan that the physical was to be perfected and taken from the earth plane for higher instruction. The perfect form could return to this earth plane to give instruction. I am not saying return as a newborn child, nor am I saying as a grown person of the flesh as you know it. I am speaking of a dimension that is far more real than the one you now live in.

My Son the Christ moved about after his resurrection in a perfected body. It was this same perfected body that he took up into the clouds and out of sight of those who stood upon the ground that day. "Out of sight" only means out of the range of the vibrations picked up by the human eye. He would not have been out of sight if they had been able to widen their range of seeing. He had only moved to a dimension that was beyond the range of the physical eye.

When I spoke of the seed that extends the life of the tree, I spoke of one physical kind of extension. Physical life is the one that is common to the earthly man. It is his way of excusing my true intention. The earthly man says, "I give life to my son or daughter, and when I die, since they are part of me as it was my seed and body that gave them life, my life is extended through them."

I said, "And in the period of rest between its seasons of fall and spring." The season of rest I spoke of was like the winter to the tree. It appears to be dead, but in truth it is very much alive. It is a simple analogy that my spiritual intention for man was to move through this life to perfection and then take that perfected body on to new responsibilities. I speak here of the spiritual man, not of the shadow or form man who has turned from me.

Sin was created by man when he turned from me, and death came into the world by sin. Since sin is created by man and death came as a byproduct of sin, you see that death is man-made and not God-made. Therefore, death is a reality of the shadow man, and since the shadow man is not real, I say that death has no reality in it at all. I speak to you in spirit and not in the terms of the earthly form.

I say to you that where the spirit dwells, all is real, all is life, and there is no death in the real or spiritual at all.

The physical man looks at death from but one dimension. He sees death as an unknown out in front of him somewhere that he approaches more closely each day. Then one final day, he stops and says, "I have not died yet, so I cannot tell you what it is, only that it is coming closer with the passing of each day."

The spiritual man who is not yet fully spiritual (unlike Jesus of Nazareth, the Christ, who was fully spiritual) sees death as a moment when he lays down his body. I am speaking of the earthly form, and his spirit then comes unto me. The spirit that comes unto me is perfected by my Spirit. Then that perfect spirit will go on to other responsibilities of a spiritual nature. This responsibility will not be as great as it could have been in terms of that spirit's working to perfect the earth and all there is upon it.

When the spirit asks of me, I answer; when the flesh or form asks of me,

I cannot answer. The spirit cannot deal in the terms of the unreal. It is why in the lesson I had you write the question twice, once as a question of the spirit man who received a true answer of my Spirit. For I am spirit, and if I was anything but real or spirit, I would not be the Creator God.

When the same question was asked the second time, it was asked by the shadow of the real man. And that same shadow gave itself the answer. When man of the flesh asks God, man himself gives forth the answer. I have said it clearly: The spirit cannot answer. The limitation is not with the Lord God; it is with the child of my love who has turned from me.

Thus saith the Lord thy God, "Knowing of the mind and spiritual knowing are not the same at all and are not to be confused one with the other." I will deal with spiritual knowing in a later lesson.

The Spiritual Quest

LESSON 7

THE NEW LIFE

I have told you before, "You must be patient and not run ahead of me. All of these matters operate by my universal laws," saith the Lord God. You, as my children, must first learn the laws and conduct yourselves by them.

Let me talk of the steps that are necessary for man to do the deeds of my Son the Christ, whom you know as Jesus of Nazareth. You have asked me of the virgin birth, and I will later deal with that matter in full detail. For now, let me continue with the truth of my unalterable law. The law is, "Whatever is given forth by man returns unto him in full measure of like kind." If you give love, it will be to you a measure of me that your filling cannot contain.

If you give out hate to any man, it will be like unto you a cancer or rapid growth that will soon find you, and you will be consumed. The law is the law, and as such, will not bend to suit your pleasure, but you will break yourself upon it if you try to live by it in any other fashion than the one of my choosing.

The First Day: The Day of Awareness

Man becomes aware that where he is and where he should be are as distant as the stars are from the sun.

Is this a conversion? It is! It is a conversion of awareness, from being unaware to becoming aware.

"Is that all there is?" you ask.

"Is life full at the day of the child's birth?" I answer.

For many of my children may come to this place where they are aware of the old and know there is a newness to be had by all. It is a new life, but life is known by living. All of life is not experienced in the summation of one day.

It is grievous to me that many of my children are content to live their lives out in that experience, which is to me but as the first day with many more in my plans for you, my children.

That one is totally dependent for the rest of his spiritual life. It is easy for that spiritual life to end by turning from me or being taken from me by his following a false call. That is but one day, and many men call it a lifetime.

You have heard it said that the first seven days are the most critical for the newborn child, and so they are. Does it not say to you if the first seven be critical for the physical child, then there must be at least six more days for the man to move into the true firmness of his spiritual birth?

The Second Day: The Inner Walk

The second day is what you now know as the inner walk. Can you not see by your own life that years can pass and the spiritual infant is living in his first day?

Can the day-old child of my Spirit do the things I have planned for him? No. He tries by prayers of repetition and a thousand acts he calls obedience to make his spiritual knowing happen. I say to you, "He cannot. It is the law." You say unto me, "But we saw prayers answered and works being done in your name." Of course, but are these the acts of a day-old child or are they being done by the father-mother God?

When the infant is wet of his making, he can but cry out. The changing and the love holding are on the part of the earthly mother and father.

That which must be done for you to have the opportunity of the second day is done by your loving Father.

The second day, as I have said, is the inner walk, for we are now talking in spiritual terms.

Again you ask, "Is it a spiritual conversion?" Of course, when man takes the inner walk, it is an act of his doing and it is a great change for him. It is but a part of the law of love being carried out to full measure.

Again he tries to do the miracles of my Son the Christ, and he says, "I know they exist and are for me to do. Why can't I do them?" In my Word, I have said that they are for all men to do to bring glory unto myself. My Son the Christ has said that even greater works than these will you do. He speaks the truth. But these things are not for the hands of the day-old child or even the two-day-old child.

The inner walk is a beautiful walk, for man begins making spiritual choices. He may choose to walk from me, and his darkness is such that he makes it harder still to come unto me.

The inner walk is followed by the outward walk.

The Third Day: The Outward Walk

The outward walk can be hours, days, weeks, or even years for the pace of the walk is set by the child. He will stop and ask questions, and I will tell him, and he may ask again and again. I will always answer for it is a part of his outward journey. He grows in his spiritual knowing as he walks.

When is the outward journey over? When he knows it has ended. There is no need to ask. If you must ask, "Is it over?", you may be sure it is not for by his asking you may know the journey is continuing still.

This third day, called the outward walk, is a great day of learning to love, for God is love, and so are you, my children, when you walk with me.

Again man tries to do the deeds of my Son the Christ, but now as this journey is complete, he has spiritual knowing. He will no longer try to do any deeds of wonder, for his journey of being has begun. And it is the dawn of the fourth day.

The Fourth Day: The Day of Being

The fourth day, called the day of being, is a day of glory indeed for the vessel has been cleansed from the inner to the outer and a great filling is about to take place.

The filling is called the filling of the Holy Spirit. When the vessel is properly prepared, the filling is full. When the vessel is not properly prepared, the full filling will not come to pass. It is the law. My law of love will return as it is given forth. Some ten, some one hundred fold will be the return. Now do you see that as the vessel is limited, so must the filling be limited and that it will not return with its fullness as it might have been?

If you would do the deeds of my Son the Christ, you must be like him. "Perfection giveth forth perfection; limitation giveth forth limitation," saith the Lord thy God. You may know where you are by what you are able to do. I speak to you of spiritual matters, for man is spirit of my Spirit.

You ask, " Is this conversion?" and I say unto you, "Yes!"

"The journey of his searching and finding is over, and his journey of his being has begun," thus saith the Lord thy God.

The Fifth Day: The Day of Planting

The fifth day is the day of planting of the seed of my seed. This is done by the Holy Spirit, for the hands of man do not touch the seed as it is planted in the man of my Spirit.

"How long does this take?" you ask, and I must ask you, "How long do you wish it to take?" It is up to you. It can be in a moment, or it may never be. That rests on your shoulders. Have I not said I rest my love upon your shoulders? So it has been said and so it has been done.

You must hold the seed so planted, for it is in this place where the being of man and the being of God the Father are becoming as one. As maturity comes, so comes responsibility.

"We hold the seed of my planting," saith the Lord thy God, "and the fifth day has come to a close."

The Sixth Day: The Day of Appearance

The sixth day is the day of appearance. There is an appearance of the plant of the spiritual planting. It is on the path of its origin. The being of man is over, and the time of growth will make of the plant a full tree in the proper season. We may say now he has become; the time of his being has ended. Behold the tree of my planting. It is as I have made it, and it is good.

"Is this a conversion?" you ask, and I answer, "Yes, for the season of the spiritual man's being is over for he has become." He does not ask any longer, "Can I now do what the Christ has done?" He can look upon the tree and see fruit, or he sees no fruit at all. When he beholds the blossom, he may know fruit will soon follow. When he sees the fruit, he will know it must grow full and unto its own ripening. He does not pick the blossom for he is no longer the child, and he knows that in the picking, he is destroying that which he seeks. Not even the fruit before its day of ripening is tempted of his picking. The child would, if lifted up, pull off the blossoms and later cry because the tree did not give its fruit when the season of giving had begun.

The Seventh Day: The Day of Harvest

The seventh day is the day of harvest. The fruit is given by the tree. It is not brought in and placed in baskets or put on the cellar steps to be sold to passers-by.

It is the seventh day, and the harvest is a day of giving. The spiritual man, who has become, has become…a giver of the fruit that is of his tree.

It was on that day that Jesus of Nazareth, the Christ, turned the water into wine. It was the needed fruit of that day.

"Is that a conversion?" you ask again and again. I say, "Yes, the spiritual man, who has become, has become a giver."

Then the fruit will be given daily as the true need occurs. How can you give truly when no need is before you? Can the vendor sell when there is no crowd? "Yea," I ask, "can he even give away his fruit when there is no one there to receive?" Then with this spiritual knowing, you must begin at the place where you find yourself.

What is all of this?

It is conversion. A man of my Spirit has returned unto me, and now he is able to do the calling for which he was made.

You wonder why I call them all conversions. The light of my presence is for all men. If he but take into his being one ray of my light, it can be called by no other word but light. If he swings wide the veil and lets my light burst in upon him in full array, it is but light. I cannot call my light in its fullness by any other word but light. So conversion is all I have said. Any light that is given to replace darkness is called conversion.

How much light will any man have?

How much would you choose to have? You may have one ray of light and live the fullness of one day in light. You may have it all and be the child of my Spirit in true fullness.

Choose ye this day!

For your review now, there are seven spiritual days: the day of awareness, the day of the inner walk, the day of the outward walk, the day of being, the day of planting, the day of appearance and the final day, the day of harvest. When these seven days have come to pass, the spiritual man is full and ready for all the spiritual tasks before him.

This lesson ends with the light before you.

The Spiritual Quest

Series Two

II

The Spiritual Quest

LESSON 8

THE KINGDOM WITHIN

Write these words.

The very word *kingdom* implies great land and holdings and subjects to do the bidding of the king.

There were followers of Jesus of Nazareth who did not understand when he spoke of the same kingdom as I now do with you. He made it clear that his kingdom was not of this world. The true kingdom of man is by its very nature a kingdom not built by human hands, nor can it be measured by the holdings of land or wealth. It is a kingdom that has no one to act as servant and is, in fact, free of all of these earthly limitations. If you were offered the space of the universe or the tiny plot of land called earth, which would you choose? If you choose the earthly and all that goes with it, you choose the limited and let the unlimited pass you by.

When my Son the Christ spoke of a kingdom, he knew it to be the realm of the spirit, which has no bounds to limit it.

The Spiritual Quest

The treasures of the universe stand ready and waiting for the man who claims this kingdom. Yet it cannot be claimed by any man of the earthly, but may be claimed by every man of the spirit.

The kingdom of which I speak is within you, and every man and woman who will look within will find it so. I am spirit, and thus, I speak in spiritual terms. Man was made boundless and free, and he was spirit of my Spirit, and his kingdom was as boundless as he was. What else could be the course of his being? Could a boundless spiritual being have anything but a kingdom of like order? If for a moment there is an end or a boundary to his kingdom, he is himself bound.

So for the physical man, the very things that make up a kingdom become the very stumbling blocks that prevent him from reaching his rightful place as my son in the spirit.

If the true kingdom of man is limitless as is the spiritual man himself, where then could this kingdom be found? If it ever has a place that can be pointed to by the fingers of men, it then has become limited and is no kingdom at all.

How then could my Son the Christ point to a place when those about him would ask him where the kingdom was? To have given them an answer that would have satisfied the realm of their asking would have reduced the real kingdom to something less than what it is. Therefore, it would have been no more a kingdom of my making for all men.

Would it not be better then for men and women to return to their place of true sonship and daughtership, and then by their returning, the kingdom of their searching will have been found.

The Kingdom Within

"Where," you ask, "do I look for this kingdom?"

Within thyself, for only at the center of man can the boundlessness for which you search be found.

You are spirit of my Spirit, and we are one when you return unto me. When you come to know our oneness as I know it now, the kingdom of which I speak will be to your knowing as well. Then you and your kingdom will be as boundless as when I first made you in the likeness of my Spirit.

Do not chase after the wise men of the world. What do they have that I have not first given you?

You have turned from me and have lost all direction for your true searching. "Stop," saith the Lord thy God, "for stopping is the first act that can bring the requests of your heart."

Let the words that follow be an instruction to your spirit.

Seek within this very hour, for the center of your own being is the place of my kingdom that knows no bounds. For when you seek within, you have by the very direction of your searching turned from all the wrong courses that have been your following.

My Son the Christ has told you that he is the way. He and I are one. Can you not see that he was directing you unto myself? My Son and I are one, and there are no divisions in oneness.

Every man that seeks me as man in the form cannot find me for I am spirit. Let the spirit of man seek after me, and he shall surely find me.

I await your coming, and you will one day know the pleasure that is mine to have you once again with me. For we are one as it has always been from the beginning.

Now do you see that my kingdom, which is for every man, does not come and go? It is where I first placed it, and it has never changed to suit the whims of physical man.

Can the shadow of the man ever stop his walking? Does not the real, when it chooses to stop, always bring the shadow under its command?

Then know this: The form of man you know as the earthly being is naught but the shadow of the real.

Can you not see the folly of it all? When in spirit you turned from me, you then gave control to the shadow and allowed it to direct your goings and your comings.

I tell you now it is your spirit that is real, and when you come unto me, you will know it. Once again, the real will direct the shadow of it, and the boundless kingdom will be yours.

Like Christ, you too are my child, even as he has said.

This lesson is finished, and your kingdom awaits you. Thus saith the Lord thy God.

LESSON 9

SONSHIP IN HIS SPIRIT

It is easy for man to understand physical sonship, and it is this understanding that blocks the man from coming to a true knowing of his own sonship in my Spirit.

The loving father gives his name and all of his possessions to his children. He could not deny them any good gift, and he will always, in his good wisdom, protect the child from the danger of his own foolish asking. The father, in love, would, at the cost of his own life, protect the lives of his great love-giving, his children.

Know this! Thus saith the Lord God, "You are my children, and you have been made in my likeness. I am spirit; therefore, your likeness must be found in the spirit of you." Do not mix the image of the real with the image of the form, or the unreal. I have said man was made in the image of God. I am spirit, and I do not speak of any other form but the spirit.

Man has lost much when he gave up his place of sonship. I did not cease to call you my son. You ceased to know by the act of your rebellion that you are indeed my true and beloved child.

All that I had first planned for you is still awaiting you. I will not – yea, I cannot – change the reality of my truth. Even if an earthly father looked upon his son and said, "He is not my own," would his saying change one hair on his son's head to that of another father? Could the son look into his father's face and say, "You are not my father," and cause to become real what the false words do declare?

Is it not easy for you to know the answers to the matters I have just addressed to you?

Then why is it so difficult for you to understand that you are my children? There are no places you can go and no words you can say that will change the reality of this truth I have just spoken.

Why does not every man know then that he is my son? He has walked from me and has clouded his own knowing with the rebellion that he calls his quest for living.

Do you remember in my Word the son who found himself eating the husks of the swine and returned to the father?

"Who was that son?" you ask.

"You are that son," is my reply. Did not that son return to the father only to find that to the father it was as if he had not been gone? He was welcomed with a glad feast that was filled with love and rejoicing.

"If you are the son of the returning, you will find I am your Father, and it will be as if you had never been gone from me," saith the Lord thy God. I am your spiritual Father, and I made you of my Spirit. I gave you form and breathed the breath of life within you, and you were to me a great joy.

What is yours when you return? All that was yours before your going. The treasures that are yours are yours still, and it will always be this way with me.

If a man has so little when he is far from me and has so much that awaits him, why has he not come unto me in great haste?

He calls his little holdings much because they are of substance like his form is substance. His far wanderings have caused him to replace his spiritual knowing with physical sensing, and thus, he compounds his own agony and delays his return unto his Father.

I have not blinded the eyes of man from my splendor. He has so turned that he no longer can behold what is his. As I have said before, can the denial of the real make it any less so for man?

Know you this now: You who read these words, you are my sons and daughters. I await your return. All that I have promised you also awaits you.

I am spirit! You are spirit of my Spirit! Let the form you know as your earthly body become subject to your spirit, and you will know that where you are and where you were made to be are as far as the pen of the swine is from the table of the father of love and truth. No words can alter this truth, and only by your returning will you know that your rightful place is among the sons and daughters of the Lord God of all creation.

"Come, my son.

"Come, my daughter.

"Come unto the joy of your Father," thus saith the Lord thy God, and thus, this lesson comes to a close.

Refresh yourself, my son, for this day has been one of great accomplishment for us both.

May you abound in my love, for I am love, and you are in me.

LESSON 10

SPIRITUAL TRUTH

Write.

Spiritual truth is truth of purest form. It is the point at which man will find no variation from the past, present, or future. It is to be the foundation of all building for the man who walks in my Spirit. Truth is what I speak to all men who seek after me.

Truth is a word that carries power to the spirits of all men.

Truth is pain to the liar, and it is revealing light to the man who does his deeds of evil under the shadows of darkness.

Truth is like the freshness of spring air that rushes into the sealed tombs of ages past and, by its very presence, causes all of its surroundings to yield to it or remain as confirmation of it. Truth is food that feeds the soul of man and clears his mind of great confusions.

Truth is an army that can make the kingdoms of man bow low, yet it lifts not its sword to destroy, but to build for every man.

The Spiritual Quest

Truth is the refreshing rain upon the mud-covered tablets of ages past that have held the newness of my Spirit as their own.

Truth is the word I speak when I tell you that you will one day find that man on this planet has been highly developed in his skills of world buildings, for he once walked this earth with the claim of his spiritual sonship upon his lips.

Let us go higher still where the mind of man cannot go, and therefore, he is unable to grasp even the slightest ray of light that comes forth as the truth of my Spirit.

My full spiritual truth is for the full spiritual man, and only this man will be able to look upon the scrolls of eternal splendor. If I were to tell you truths of my higher spiritual knowing, you would but wonder if these could be the words of man. Yes, I say you would pull them down from their rightful spiritual place in order to examine them more closely, and in so doing, they would have lost their true value. The truth of the spirit is truth for the spirit only, and the physical man cannot hold it in his hands. It is like the wind in his face; he knows of its presence, but cannot contain his knowing.

Spiritual truth is to be the instruction for the child who knows he is of me. Then this great tool of my giving becomes the tool of his shaping.

Would you go to your moon and gather her rocks if you knew the moon to be nothing more than a former part of the earth that now has become a shelter for holding your own limited knowing of the truth? You will one day discover this to be true, and then the grandeur of it all will be reduced to what it is in truth.

Spiritual Truth

The stars are the steppingstones for the man of my Spirit, and he has but to come unto me for the spiritual truth to be a part of his own knowing.

Do you believe earthly man to be the highest creature of my making when I have repeatedly told you that earthly man has no reality at all? It was a spiritual man I placed upon this earth, and he walked in my truth, and his deeds, if told unto you, would cause the earthly man to resist the truth of them.

Through my Son the Christ, I spoke spiritual truths, and your resistance put him upon a cross. "Seek first my kingdom, and I shall add all other things" is a truth of my Spirit. You have made of it a motto to hang upon your wall rather than to truly first seek my kingdom for fear that all things might indeed be yours.

Oh! You say you wish to serve me, and you sing praises unto my name. Do you not know that when our spirits are one, you have but to speak my name softly, and the seas will calm at the raising of your hand? The mountains will move and become valleys and plains of great richness. All this is truth to the spiritual child of my deepest love.

Who then could this child be? You! You are this child. That is a spiritual truth.

"Oh, if only it were so," say the men of the earth.

"Oh, it is so," says the man of the spirit.

"Which of these two sighs come forth from you? Then you may know where you stand on this lesson of spiritual truth which has just been shared with you," saith thy God. I speak truth, and naught but truth can

I speak for I am that which I speak.

I praise you, O God!

I bless you, O my son!

LESSON 11

SPIRITUAL REFRESHMENT

Are you prepared to write?

Yes, Lord.

I know, and it pleases me that you grow stronger each day. I am the source of that strength which allows you to speak with boldness. Walk the path of assurance. Write the truths that are of my Spirit and face all men around you and give forth my love. I will not allow more to come upon you during these days of rapid growing.

These matters that I have just spoken are the results of spiritual refreshment.

Just as you feed the body with proper care and food so that it remains strong and active, likewise does the spirit of man become strong and remain in that strength when properly fed.

There is nothing the physical man can do to produce the food needed to sustain his spirit. The two are as far as the east is from the west, and therefore, the labor of man is in vain. Have I not said unto you it will produce naught but dust mingled with sweat and tears?

As you are now coming to know man, true man is a spiritual being made of my love, and the earthly form or body is nothing more than the shell that makes it possible to live in the physical plane I call love's manifestation. I made you all that you are, and I hold you by my Spirit, for in spirit we are one.

As you plant the seed and work the soil, in time you will have food in a place where there was no food before. This does not seem strange to you for you have come to know that the seed of the physical, when planted and cared for, will produce of its own kind and that it will nourish the body. And all this is to my pleasure since it was of my origin in giving to man all the means to sustain his physical life.

Would it not seem strange, then, that I would so carefully have planned a way of physical sustaining without having a plan for the spiritual sustaining of the spiritual man? Of course I have provided a perfect plan for the spiritual man of my creative love.

The spiritual man is of eternal value, while the physical man is of the dust and is but a manifestation of the real man.

You ask, "Then when does the spiritual man begin his refreshment? What does it consist of?" Man's spiritual feeding begins when he knows he is of a spiritual origin, and he of his own choosing gives the proper value to matters of the spirit. It would be a waste to put a spiritual meal before a man who is conscious only of the physical. He would walk past the food of real value to get to matters of physical choosing.

Spiritual Refreshment

It is like placing two baskets before the child, one filled with great treasure and the other filled with brightly colored wrappings with treasure of little value. The child will pass the true treasure to reach for the things that are pleasing to the eye.

You are my children, and for centuries you have, for the most part, passed up the real to reach for illusion and dust. It is in love that I have made you, and I shall never leave you. I wait for the day when you come to know true value and then reach for matters of eternal value. The day will come, and these lessons that are now being given forth from me will help many find their refreshment of the spirit.

As to the matter of refreshment itself, let it be clearly known that only eternal substance is worthy of feeding the spiritual man.

I give a refreshment of spiritual rest, and the daily awakening finds your spirit truly rested. This is the food of eternal peace that can only flow from the Father.

The physical man at the end of his day of turmoil finds no place to lay his head in peace; thus, his sleep is not restful.

"Rest in me," saith the Lord thy God, "and I will give you a place within that shall make every fiber of your being know a true rest."

When the spirit of man is at peace within, the form of man is at rest without.

I tell you now that joy is a spiritual food, and it is one that is filling and long sustaining. It is food that fills and lifts man above the chaos of his surroundings. Then, and only then, can man deal with the chaos itself and not be caught up by it. The spiritual man with the refreshment of joy is then able to share what he has become, and the chaos of his surroundings will be changed to one of joy because of his spiritual sharing.

The beggar with a few crumbs of bread in his tattered pocket is not able to set a feast for his brother for he must first have before he can then give. How then could a man with no joy within give joy to his fellow men around him? He does not. He cannot. Joy is food of the spirit, and the child of my Spirit can set a feast before his brothers, and there will be enough for all to be fed who will come to the table. I have said it. I am that which I give forth unto every man, and you are what you give forth unto every man. Refresh your spirit in me, and you will have much refreshment to share with your brother and sister.

Love is a feeding of my Spirit. I speak of the spiritual and not of the physical. They are not to be confused one with the other. My spiritual love is given forth and is by its very nature a food that sustains the spirit of man. It sustains because once given, it is never drawn away. It is an ever-flowing forth of me. When you feast upon my love, you will thrill in your spirit for it is a vibration that thrills the soul, body, and spirit.

Love is a healer of a full and perfect nature. I am your God. I have made you by my loving, and it shall always be.

When you return to me and become the spiritual being of my original making, you will be filled with me, and then you will be able to give forth my love to all around you.

The spiritual man who feasts at my table of refreshment will be filled

Spiritual Refreshment

indeed, and therefore, you will have much filling to give to all my children who do not yet know they may come to the table of refreshment and be filled to overflowing.

These are not all of my foods of spiritual refreshment, but when you have feasted upon these, you will be ready for more of my spiritual giving.

This lesson is for every man who will come unto me and be filled by my spiritual food for his spirit. Thus saith the Lord thy God.

The Spiritual Quest

LESSON 12

SPIRITUAL LIGHT

Man knows very little of my light, and his sensing is even less of a reliable source for him to use for his understanding.

I am light. I am spirit. It is I who lighteth the path of every man. Man must walk in the spirit before he may come to know the meaning and the value of what I call spiritual light.

You must now let go of all that you hold to as a physical man if you are to grasp the true meaning of these words.

Man has so ingrained his knowing with a false understanding of light that it is his very false knowing that prevents him from coming to the true light that is for every man. It is as if it is light that keeps man from coming to the true light. This being so, does it not say to you that which man now holds to be light must in fact be a false light and, therefore, is no light at all? My Son the Christ has said, "I am the light of the world," and so he was, and so he is, and so he will be forever.

It was something that was not for him alone, but for every man. Christ was the fullness of my light and, therefore, was able to give to every man the offer of a full measure.

He could only offer light to men as he does this day, even as I now offer my light to you and, through you, to every man.

Know now that the offer was of a spiritual nature. Therefore, many men took the offer as some kind of physical matter, and thus, they did not understand. They rejected the very offer to that which would have allowed them to move from physical darkness into spiritual light.

Again I say, "I am light, and I am spirit." Seek me in spirit, and you will find and walk in the light of my presence. Light is not for the physical man because never has the real been designed or offered to the unreal.

Let me now clearly give you some truths that will help in your understanding.

Light is a vibration of my Spirit, and it is a vibration that I have used to make all that you now know as the physical world. One day, your people of science will come to know that all matter can be reduced to light. They will think their discovery is all there is to the reality of light, but they could not be further from the truth.

Oh, if you would only come unto me quickly so no more ages would slip through your fingers, and you would become the creatures of light that in love I made you to be.

Which will it be for you today – the darkness of man you call light or the light of my Spirit for the spiritual man's using?

LESSON 13

THIS AGE'S WISDOM

Are you prepared to write?

Yes, my spirit is ready.

This age of which I speak is one that shall bring the light of my Spirit into the corners of the darkness of the old age. When the new has arrived fully, the old will soon be gone. This true new age that stands on the threshold will soon be ready to step forth in full grandeur, for it is the age of the spiritual man.

By his power, the spiritual man will cause the old to crumble into dust. By his love, he will lift all men and women around him to new heights as only love can display. By his words, he will speak the wisdom of the spirit that makes the words of the physical man sound empty and hollow.

It will be as I have said, that out of the mouth of babes in me will come forth the wisdom of which I speak. A child of mine who moves and has his being in the presence of the Lord God will speak with such clarity that the earthly man must turn a deaf ear if he is to resist the forthcoming truth.

It is to be an age of new values, and he who continues to strive after the old will be called foolish indeed.

No longer will a man act upon the guesswork of those around him for he will call upon his own spiritual knowing. His every act will work to perfection. He will not know loss of substance or energy, and all around him will also be blessed by his activity.

Men will lift their fellow men in love and teach the truths that make all men free in spirit, for only then is man truly free at all.

Your strides in science and all related matters will be great, for the spiritual man strives for the uplifting of his downtrodden brother. The burden of greed will be lifted, for it has never made a stronger man or nation. It has been a deceiver of great proportion and always a destroyer of the very ones who gave unto greed its energy to exist at all.

Is it not an act on the part of the wise to share his best knowing with his brother? For it may well be that his knowing will be of a lift to you as well.

When is it I have said that color or race or nations are to be turned upon and called by any other word than love? Man of the earth has made divisions where there were none and has called some good and some bad according to his own choosing.

I have said the man of the earth cannot enter the kingdom of God. It is a spiritual matter and not a physical one. Even in this, my love goes

This Age's Wisdom

forth and waits upon the return of the rebellious ones. I love them no less than you; only by their rebellion from me do they make my love ineffective within them.

Is it not wise to live in the world of the real and give no value to the world of shadows, illusions, false promises, and, finally, dust? This is the wisdom of which I speak: the wisdom of the spiritual age.

Men will use their lost and sensitive powers that were given for the use of the spiritual man. The earthly man has no knowing of the things I now speak and has no use of the real powers of the true man.

Which is the act of the wise man, to share new ways to destroy his fellow man or to work to build a better world for all men?

Every man was made to be free. I do not speak of slave and free man, for neither of these earthly men are free. One is bound by chains, and the other is bound even more tightly in his mind by false truths, and thus, both are slaves to false masters.

The freedom of which I speak is for the spiritual man alone, and not until your own knowing tells you the truth of the freedom of my giving will you be free men indeed.

As long as one mouth is hungry for food, all of man is starving, for every man is brother of every other.

"How shall we feed all the starving of this world?" you quickly ask, and I answer, "Never will man of the earth feed all the earthly man." Men of my Spirit have never known starvation for it does not exist in the realm that I made for the spiritual man. Is it not in a new wisdom that men and women are led to know their origin and call themselves the sons and daughters of God? I then will direct their paths, and their abundance will be of my making, and they will live in the riches of my grand and glorious kingdom.

Tell me what would this world be if it were a world that seeks after me? "Like a heaven," you say. "And thus was my intention for you," is my reply.

The wisdom of this age will not discover new truths for there are none called new. Only to the finder who did not know them are they so called. Truth will be the discovery, and where truth is, falseness cannot be found.

Your books of learning will reflect the new, and the old will be used to measure only the distance of man's earlier fall. Even now you look upon relics of the past age with delight and humor for the changes have been great.

I ask you now, "Why have you perfected so well the relics of your delight and humor? Have you not compounded the error so the next age can look upon your relics with the same spirit of delight?"

Why not in my Spirit use a method of the true new age to simplify what is already before you?

Can you now see that anything which man uses up in due time and which destroys his surroundings in the process is not in the hands of the wise?

The wisdom of the spiritual man will use that which is as usable when he is finished as it was before he used it. I speak to you in parable, so in speaking, the physical man can become the spiritual once again. Nothing in the nature of my creation takes without giving equally as much in return. Only physical man is the taker and the user and does not give in return. Can you see that he only destroys himself in the process of his taking?

Be wise men in this age of fools.

Be spiritual men in this age of men of darkness and shadows.

Be loving men in this age that will be changed by love.

Be giving men, for in so giving, you truly receive.

Be children of my Spirit, and through you will the wisdom of the age come forth.

I have spoken these words in truth and love for I am that which I speak. I am the Lord thy God.

The joy within you now confirms what I have said unto all men.

Thus this lesson is concluded.

The Spiritual Quest

LESSON 14

ALL KNOWING

Are you ready?

Yes, Father.

I would begin with a parable of seed and a sower. There is a knowing in the mind of the sower that when the seed is planted and cared for properly, it will reproduce itself and yield manyfold. That is in the mind of the sower, and to him, it is all that he needs to raise his crops.

A man of agriculture visits the farmer and asks if he might take some of the seed to see if he can find a deeper knowing about the seed. With his study, soon he finds new and better methods to raise crops of that seed.

A third man comes and is a man of science of the deepest order. He then gathers some of the seed from the second man, and he comes to still a deeper knowing from all the rest. "Ah," says he, "now we truly know."

A child comes along and takes some grain from the man of science. He puts the grain in his mouth, chews and chews, and smiles as he walks along enjoying the grain of the three men.

When knowing was complete, did not the child still have yet another knowing as valid as the three before him?

I am God, and I am all knowing. Everything that man has ever known or will ever know is already clear in my knowing.

Just when you are about to say, "Now I really know," a child will come along and add much to your ending, which was not an ending at all.

Man as the earthly being he claims to be will never be all knowing. Man as the spiritual being I claim him to be will be no less than all knowing.

"How," you ask, "can man be all knowing?" When he is one in my Spirit, then we are truly one, and I keep nothing from him.

Every need of his searching is found as he begins; every request of his spirit is granted at the asking. All knowing that is to his reaching is within his grasp. "Does every man of the spirit know all?" you ask of me. I answer, "Whatever his need will be his supply. Would you carry the pack of the mountain climber to swim in the waters of the sea?" "No," you reply, "I carry what is needed for the task." Then select the task of your spirit, and you will be so equipped.

Again let me say the king is a very rich man and he has chests full of treasure, gold coins by the ton, and much silver beyond his counting.

As he goes about his kingdom, does he carry all of his treasure upon his back to show his wealth through the kingdom?

If he tried, would it not be the voice of a child that would say, "There

All Knowing

goes a donkey dressed up like our king"?

O my son, do you now know and, in knowing, cease to ask the questions that have little eternal value?

When you are one with me, all that I know is yours as well. For with every spiritual question, there comes forth the answer, and it is one of truth.

It is for another lesson to talk of the method employed by the spiritual man to bring into physical reality the matter of his spiritual knowing. Let it be said now that what I have said is for the spirit man, so it would be good for you to make haste to come unto me. The delay is with you, and the loss that you sustain by your delay is equal to the true value of what I have for you. Let me illustrate.

_____

_____

_____

I have asked you to leave a space of three lines. I say to you there are matters that are ready for the knowing of spiritual man, but physical man is not now, nor will he ever be, ready for these matters.

Words will one day go in place of the space above.

For now you may look at that blank space and say, "GOD IS ALL KNOWING!" and it is truth you speak.

When you look at that blank space and say, "GOD IS ALL KNOWING!" and know it to be true, then you, not I, will fill in the missing words above.

"How do I get there?" you ask.

"Come unto me," I answer.

This lesson and this second series have come to a close.

"Prepare yourself for more words of my Spirit," saith the Lord thy God.

It is finished; it is but the beginning.

The Spiritual Quest

Series Three

III

The Spiritual Quest

LESSON 15

OLD TREASURES IN NEW CANVAS

Are you prepared, my son?

Father, you know the flutter within.

There is peace in my Word, and now I say unto you, be at peace in this matter at hand that is before you. It is all in my handling. If you have not that assurance, how can we proceed with other matters of greater significance?

Good. Now for the matter at hand.

The treasures of my Spirit are the treasures that await man upon his return to his true spiritual self. The treasures that I offer are internal in nature and will, therefore, sustain you throughout the eternity that is before every man.

My Word is a treasure for every man who will give ear to my truth and, having heard, takes within the truth of his hearing.

Has man learned to feed without the intake of food? Though there is such a way, it is not yet to the knowing of most men. Then the value for man will be raised as he takes within and makes as his own the word of my offering. If man be changed in his value, has he not then taken within a treasure of great value?

Is there any weight of gold or silver, even if measured in tonnage, that will change the value of its owner? The external cannot change the internal. The physical cannot change the spiritual. It is the spiritual that changes the value of the physical.

Is there any eternal value in canvas, or does it in time change until the weight of one coin has made it useless and, therefore, of no value? Is it not also true that once discarded, it is but a brief time more and it has vanished into dust?

Is not man's body form as lasting as the canvas? Then do you see the value of the treasure lies in the treasure itself and not in its container?

My love is a treasure of eternal value. Have I not said my love is for every man? It will always be as I have said. I will not take away the offer of this treasure to man.

Does not the canvas carry what is placed within it? Can it carry any treasure that is not found within its boundary? Then love, like my Word, must be taken within. It will follow every man and will be with him awaiting his reception at every turn. He can run to the far corners of the earth and, without breath and with great tire, fall to his knees, only to find his fall has been cushioned by my love that awaits him. It is, by its very nature and being, an ever-present offer of great, eternal value to man.

Why not this day allow me to come within you? You will love even now as you are loved.

There is yet another treasure among many that I would lift up now for you to see more clearly, and thus seeing, you may place it within the fold of your canvas which you indeed are.

That treasure is life eternal. I first said it, and it has been repeated ever since by man of the earth.

You say life eternal is that which follows after death. I say there is no death at all.

Quickly man says, "I can tell you by name some who are dead and buried."

I say, "Death came into the world through sin, and sin is the creation of man. If sin is man's creation and death its offspring, then it too is a creation of man." Since the physical man is not the real, then all of his handiwork is as he is. It is a truth, then, that the matters made by earthly man are like he is and therefore, there is no reality in any of them.

Let us first make a division between the earthly man who sinned and became as I have just said – earthly – and the spiritual man of my creation whom I love. That which I have made is out of myself and, therefore, must be eternal as I am eternal.

You ask me, "Did you not make an earthly man?" I must answer you by saying that I made a spiritual man in my likeness whose manifest form was a physical man of this earth. There is a great deal of difference between an earthly man, who through sin has turned from me and has separated himself from all that is real, and a man of the earth who is spirit of my Spirit.

Now let me tell you of my plan for man regarding the matter of death. It has not changed from the origin of its conception to this moment. Death is not now, nor has it ever been, in my plan for man. I say unto you if man had not sinned, he would never have known there to be such a possibility for his choosing. I would have had man be born and manifested into physical form, grow and mature, and, when perfected, bring himself unto me for matters of higher spiritual knowing.

Yes, write that I am saying I had planned that man never know of death.

It is even now true that the spirit of man does not die. Man the real, man the true, man the spiritual does not die; he cannot die. Again I say death is a creation of your limitation, not of my doing.

Do you now understand that the form was to be perfected and taken with you for higher matters? This is what you have recorded of Jesus of Nazareth, the Christ. He perfected his physical form by giving the spirit full control, thus having a oneness in fullness in me. What he did with his earthly form was what I had intended all men to do. Thus, do you now see that he is truly the way for all men? Man is such that when he comes to a higher knowing, he will then see that what was done for him by example was done so one day he could also do that same act. The weak physical man has for centuries excused himself from his true spiritual place by saying it was the act that only a son of God could do. This is a truth. I say, "Who are you but a son or a daughter of God? Is not this truth also found in my Word given to earlier prophets?"

Do you mean…

Yes, I do mean that you are to be like my Son the Christ. He was fully man, and he was fully God. You all say this with ease.

I say unto you, "Let the Lord God speak now to your spirit."

Pattern your life like the way of the pattern: Christ.

Claim your sonship, as did he.

Know that your claim is the truth of my Word.

Live with every breath you breathe the reality of your knowing.

Proclaim the reality that you live.

Become what it is you proclaim. For in becoming, you will find that now you, too, are a part of the way for another to come unto me.

Christ is the way.

I do not mean for all men, then, to only praise the way without becoming a part of the way.

Which is a better praise: for you to utter words that give glory to the way for all men or for you to live out the example that is given to you by Christ my Son, the way for every man?

It is like he has built a grand and glorious highway that, if traveled, would bring the traveler to me.

What have you done these two thousand years but stand alongside of the road casting love petals upon it when it was built for man to walk upon?

"Oh, I dare not walk upon that road," you say, "for it would not give honor to the Galilean of love."

"Walk the road," I say. "Yea, run upon it!" He will call you brother, and you will be met by arms outstretched, and you will see him as he is this day. For He is alive; he lives this day. In the perfect form of the physical, he lives. For he is spirit of my Spirit, and in him is no death at all. And I speak both of the physical and the spiritual.

Now do you see some of the value of this treasure?

Then this day, place it within the canvas. For it is a treasure beyond value, as are all the rest. This lesson has ended, but the teaching of it is only about to begin.

O my God in heaven.

I am all that you speak and still more.

Rest now, for tomorrow there is great joy for you to feast upon.

LESSON 16

THE SERVICE OF THE SCRIBE

"Write, for the words are not your own, but the words of my Spirit speaking unto your spirit," saith the Lord thy God.

Men will ask you why and how you were used to be a scribe unto the Lord. You should not give an answer for the why and how were of my choosing and not of your own.

The prophet will speak on matters of my doing, and again it is my Spirit that speaks unto his spirit, and thus, he points unto the plans of my Spirit on earth.

The scribe allows the words of my Spirit to speak to his spirit, and thus, my words for this age are brought forth. It is true that some will reject these words of my Spirit, but this has been so with man from the early days of his fall. There are many men and women who are prepared in their spirits for these, my words, and will take them to heart and, thus, find the food of nourishment for their spirits.

The Spiritual Quest

I will now answer the questions of the true spirit who asks how and why in order that he or she, too, may become a scribe for my Spirit.

If the questions are asked in any other form but that of a searching spirit, there is no answer at all. I say unto you, "Let man himself answer his own questions for if he were given a true spirit answer, it would be but rejected, and he would fashion an answer to his own satisfaction." Spirit does not deal in matters of the flesh; I cannot. I wait for the spirit of man to turn back unto me, and then all the questions of his heart will find their answers.

The question why is already clear to the spirit one of my love, for it gives me joy to give forth my words again, fresh and anew, to the searching spirits of my children. Thus, man can once again know that this is an age when I will speak, and the deeds of my Spirit will once again be seen before men.

When the Scriptures were given (both the Old Testament and the New as well as many other words given through my spirit scribes), it was not intended that man would stop all efforts to continue to hear from me. I would have given you words of great power and assistance through the ages, but for the most part, limited men of mind and spirit chose to use only what was given through my prophets and scribes at that time. Was the spirit-filled man of that age any different from the spirit-filled man of this age? Would you have men believe that I could speak through the scribes of that age, and then for two thousand years and more, I have had nothing to say or have chosen to remain silent? Does a father of love so act toward his children? Or does he give his words of love and infilling daily to his sons and daughters?

No, I say unto you as your God and father-mother of your true spirit, I would have spoken daily if men would have allowed their spirits to be receptive unto my Spirit.

When I answer the question of how this is done this day, I will tell you I have not changed. Man changed, and his change has cost him these years of silence.

The scribe of my choosing must come to a place where his searching has ended in his encounter with my Spirit. His period of rebellion has ended, and he stands at the end of his turning from me. He then turns unto me in fullness of trust of his spirit.

It takes a truly bold spirit to write, "Thus saith the Lord thy God," for these are words that have been reserved for a special few. This is the opinion of limited men. The truth of the boldness is before you, but they are not words for a special few as "Thus saith the Lord" is spoken.

Every man or woman, when he or she comes to his or her full knowing, will know that he or she is my son or daughter of my Spirit, and I am ready to speak my truth unto every man of the spirit. As it has always been, I have nothing to say to the earthly or fleshly man for the Spirit speaks to the spirit, just as you know the fleshly man may speak to the flesh, but has nothing to say to the spirit of man or God. The two ways are as far apart as the very power of the words given forth by the earthly against the spirit.

The scribe of my Spirit must be willing to keep his own feelings and words to one side so they may not be expressed at all, that is to say, until we are fully one. At that time, the words he writes will be from me as well as from himself for the oneness will have been made complete.

When I first spoke to this scribe, he placed the words of my Spirit upon the paper, but he reacted in awe and fear, and thus, many days passed before we could speak together. In those days, the scribe of my Spirit spent himself in searching for the truth, and he kept himself an open vessel. This must be done by all who would write the words of my Spirit.

The scribe must grow to a place where he is ready for my words to go forth unto all men. It will be at that time a blessing of great joy, but it will be a time of much question on the part of many men. They will ask questions while the true questions of their minds will be held in reserve. They will say, "Who is he to so receive these words?" They will of a truth be asking, "Why have I not had such words come through me?"

The scribe has no need of answering for I will always speak through him and I will always answer the true question whether it be spoken or not. I will always answer in the spirit for the Spirit speaks to the spirit. I will always answer in love for I am that which I answer.

I say unto you who would be a scribe of my truth, "Prepare your spirit so we may become one, and I will speak through you as well." I have no special love for this scribe above that of any other of my children. Are not you all my children?

I will speak my words of truth wherever I find the vessel so prepared for my using. We are not lifting up the scribe because of what comes forth from me through him. We lift up the spirit-to-spirit truth for what it can bring forth to all men. In the days of the writing of the spirit-filled men, there were those around them who cried out, "Who are you to say, 'God has spoken through me'?" As long as you have men who have turned their lives over to the flesh, you will hear those empty and hollow cries.

You are but to give them my love and truth. Then the task of the scribe has ended in this matter of this lesson of spiritual learning.

The Spiritual Quest

LESSON 17

SPIRITUAL HUMILITY IN A ROYAL ROBE

Are you prepared?

Yes, Father.

Then write these words so men may have a clear understanding of this matter. The kingdom of the spirit is the only kingdom where reality may be found, and as sons and daughters of my loving Spirit, you must now know the royal robe is for every child. There are none created who are not my sons and daughters. Man, the physical that you now know to be only the shadow of the real, has taken my words of truth and set up kingdoms that have no reality in them at all. Then from time to time, he has selected one of his own to rule this kingdom of shadows. If man is set to rule, there must be someone placed beneath the king, lest his rule would be without a subject. It was in the sin and weakness of man that such rules were established, and I have never had a hand in such matters.

Why then, you ask, have I spoken of a royal robe and now speak about a kingdom of the spirit?

It is so that every man will come to a new and true understanding of the true place for man. "If every child is born for a royal robe, then who are to be the subjects of this kingdom?" you ask. There are none that are subject one unto another, for then the kingdom of which I speak would be no better than those established by sinful man. My kingdom is boundless and free, and every man is ruler of the full domain of my giving. All matters are then in proper order, and there can be no confusion or chaos in a kingdom of perfect order. I speak of the true and the real, for the kingdom of my establishment is a spiritual one. Thus, the royal robe is for every man and woman for every man and woman are my manifest love in a full expression. With every man a king and every woman a queen, it is then a grand and royal kingdom indeed.

In the kingdoms of men, there are many servants that surround the royal family and wait upon them at their every bidding. I have said in the spiritual halls where the royal robes are found, all are so regally dressed. Do you now see that every man, if he is to be so clothed, is not placed above another by it? I tell you now a truth that has never been known to the kingdoms of man. Every child so royally clothed is a servant unto every other. I have told you this was a matter of spiritual humility in a royal robe. That is not at all like the kingdoms of men.

You now know the kingdom of the real is spiritual, and the kingdoms of man are no more than the shadows of the sundial that man used to tell the time of day. For by the time the king made the request of time and a return from the dial had been made, the shadow that gave the answer to his seeking was gone like the passing of his own kingdom.

Spiritual Humility in a Royal Robe

Spiritual humility is the serving act of the child of the spirit. Man has acted so foolishly in the matter. He has called himself humble by folding his hands and giving the utterances of many words that he believes to be pleasing to my ears and the ears of his surroundings. The spirit of the humble child, who is servant of all around him, is one with my Spirit and knows there are no needs that are met by words from the physical man.

Only the spirit can cause, by the use of words, a manifest form to be. Only the spirit can cause the real to be before the eyes of the earthly child.

Now you can see clearly the royal robe is the one worn by the servant of his fellow man.

Jesus of Nazareth was and is and always will be my Son of full spirit. He wears the royal robe of which I speak, and he is servant to every man even unto this day. His work is more active now than ever before.

The earthly man will quickly say, "I cannot see him. Why do you say his work is more active?" I ask you, has the earthly man ever seen matters of the spirit? Has he ever understood the meaning of the royal robe as one of servant wearing? Does he ever speak words of humble origin and have a true knowing that his speaking has caused anything to be changed? The teaching of the earthly man can be no better than he is. He is limited, and thus, his teachings carry all of his limitations.

I say the royal robe is for all, and man says the royal robe is for but one man. I say the man in the royal robe is to serve, and man says he is to be served. I say he is to be humble, and man says he is to say words that sound humble. I speak unto you in full truth so you may learn and accept your true place of grandeur by my side. Man speaks words without truth, and he places the robe of royalty upon the shoulders of a king of an earthly kingdom. When that king is placed within the ground, man then places the robe upon the shoulders of another and says, "The king is dead. Long live the king!" I say unto you the king lives! Long live the king, for he can never die. You are the king of my speaking, and these words are for every man.

If you would be my king, then serve all men under the direction of my Spirit. Do not fold your hands and speak words, but extend your hands in service unto another and be the spirit of my Spirit, and you shall hear my Spirit's words spoken from the mouth of God.

As much as Christ is the way for every man, he is the truth. His life, deeds, and words have proclaimed his knowing, and he wears the royal robe of my giving.

Come unto me, spirit sons and daughters, for your kingdom of service awaits you. Walk humbly in the path of my choosing, and you will have the garden walk with the Lord thy God.

I have thus spoken the truth for your edification, and the lesson has ended so your service may begin.

LESSON 18

THE NATURE OF GOD

As I speak to you now, you must surely know that I would give my truth directly to every child of my love if they would but prepare themselves for me. I am a loving father, and I would share all of my wealth-giving with every child of my making. It is the turning of man that has caused our separation. For me, the spiritual man that I made you to be has not gone from my presence. It is only your form, called body, that says there is distance between us, and after speaking thus, you place these false words in your knowing, and thus, you seek to make real the unreal by your own rebellious acts. Have I not said that the body form, or earthly man, cannot effect any change at all upon spiritual matters? I tell you in spirit you have not gone from me at all, and the Spirit of God and your true spirit are now as one. Even as those words are given as they were the day of my making and giving, know it to be true.

Does it seem strange to you now for me to say I am present with you even now? Only your knowing is keeping this truth from being a reality to you as it is a reality to me. I am God, and by my very nature, what I do, I do not change. If I were to change anything from my original plan, it would make of me less than I am, and therefore, it cannot be.

I hear the question of your spirit even as I give you these words above. Yes, there are places where it is recorded in my Word given unto prophets of old that men of great spirit cried unto me, and earthly elements changed because of their crying forth. It is true that these things happened, and it will soon be true that you will know that you, too, can call forth of me and cause the elements to yield to your call.

"Let it be known now unto all men," saith the Lord thy God, "when the elements that surround you are affected by your request, I have but given you the power to deal with the elements of the physical." I have made it quite clear that you, man of my love and spirit, are ruler of all you survey. The earthly world is under the control of the man of my Spirit, made into flesh, of this very same earth he wishes to rule. When you are spirit man, you have but to make clear your request. And while the asking is being done, the answer of the gift is then forthcoming. You have then but to bring down into the physical plane the request of your spirit. If you truly have need for the sun to stand and hold its rays of giving longer than is usual for its natural course, know that it will be done. The spiritual man does not make folly of such power, so it could not be done in idle jest. If it were so, the request would surely destroy the requester before I would allow the universe to be affected by some foolish request. It is for this very reason the matters and powers of the spirit are held for the true spiritual being and are not found within the reach of the physical man, whom I call but the shadow of the real.

I am present within you when your knowing becomes clear to the truth

The Nature of God

of which I speak. My presence brings within the man all the attributes that I am; therefore, man himself with his true knowing has the assurance that what I speak is the truth for all eternity.

When I am fully present within you, the others around you who are of a seeking nature and who are spirit of my Spirit will also know of my presence within you. They will join with you in your rejoicing. Man of the flesh, who knows not of what I speak, will continue on in his walk of blindness. He is tapping his cane or reaching forth his hand and says, "I can see clearly now, but there is nothing before me that is to be seen."

My presence within man will make many changes moment by moment as he grows in me. He will become a tree of great planting, and his branches will reach to all corners of the earth. The fruit of his branches will be sweet unto all men, and he will heal at the speaking of my name. He has but to ask, and the treasure of his asking will stand before him ready to be used.

All the spiritual qualities that are of me, by nature, become the property of my spiritual son or daughter.

Do you not see that I am saying all that I have, you shall have; all that I am, you shall become; and all that is part of my very being is prepared and waiting to become your being as well?

Can you find any word that I did not speak for your good?

Can you find any gift that was not of perfection and made for your person of the spirit?

Can you find a place for man to go where he will not find me there waiting for his return?

Can you find any reason for not knowing that I am within you and have never moved from that place? Know now that only your limited knowing and acceptance of this truth keep us apart even now.

I am God. I am ever present in all of my creation. Man is the greatest love of my creation. I am ever present in man.

I speak the truth, and your calling it by any other word will not change it. Why not now accept me and call me Father, for such I am to every man?

How close am I to you? I am within you.

When will you know this to be the truth?

When will you accept me as your Creator God?

How will you know it is I who speak and not the voice of your own mind? The mind of man is the highest climb man can make on his own strength. When he has climbed to that place, he will know that these words come forth from a source that is beyond his own grasping.

When are you to accept this presence? Whenever you wish, I await your coming unto me.

And if you refuse to come unto me? I will await your coming. The agony of your waiting is of your own making. And again I say, "Come unto me. I am thy God. I am ever present."

We are finished for now with this matter, and thus, the lesson is opened.

LESSON 19

GOD'S HEALING LOVE

This subject is far deeper than man supposes it to be.

When I speak of healing, I speak in spirit of spiritual healing, and it is my love that is given forth in constant measure that allows the spiritual healing of man to take place. If you knew all the details of this accomplishment and worked with me for them to become a reality in the real spiritual being which you are, with all this there would be no change in the physical body.

There are further steps to be taken by the spiritual being for the physical being or form to know a healing within itself. It is then, in this order, the healing takes place in man. My love draws man back unto me, he gives the spirit control, and true spiritual healing takes place within the spiritual being. The spiritual being then affects the changes necessary for the form to know a complete healing.

Man has everything within himself to know a complete physical healing, but it is accomplished first on the spiritual level and then carried on into the physical realm where the shadow of the real dwells. With this clear in your knowing, let me now explain each step necessary to help the physical.

Let me begin with an understanding of love that will help you, each and every one. Every giving of my Spirit has a vibration to it. Each of these vibrations is within the full range of the spiritual man and is outside of the narrow range of earthly man's sensing. Earthly man can know my love, but it comes through his sense of knowing, which is a spiritual sense. It is when man has turned back unto me that his lost sense of knowing once again begins its activity and he begins to know my love. The vibration of my love is at a rate that man is drawn unto me as long as he is turned toward me. When he turns away from me, he rejects the drawing of my love and moves still farther from me. I am love, and where the presence of my love vibration is found, there I am.

Healing is, as you know it, a total vibration of every part of the same man. If you are injured in form, then various vibrations of those parts of your body that are injured, moment by moment, rebuild the broken or injured part of the form. It is how I first made man, only I made him for a complete and instant healing. It is man's rejection of me that has taken him far from me and my full method of healing. The medications that man now uses are but aids and substitutes for the real and intended method of my healing.

Let us now speak of the result of my love vibration upon the real, or the spiritual, man who returns unto me. Have I not said that we are to be one, even as Jesus of Nazareth has said unto you, "I and the Father are one"? It was a truth when he spoke it, and it is a truth prepared for every man of the spirit. When the real spirit, who you are, and I have become one, the vibration of my love becomes the vibration of your spirit as well. I intended this to be the condition of every man. When we are one, then the vibrations of which I speak are also in that same oneness. The spiritual man is then truly healed in every sense and in every way. Still at this place, the form is unchanged. The spirit must first be healed before my healing can take place in the form. Then the spirit of you, which is the real, begins its control of the earthly form or shadow. The speed of the physical healing is dependent upon the condition of the spirit affecting the healing of the form. When you are fully one with me, then the form is instantly healed. However, when your spirit has just begun its change back to oneness, it will take more time, as you know it, for the form to be healed.

Jesus of Nazareth, my Son the Christ, was in the fullness of me, and so his healing was at the same level of perfection.

Now let me speak to the matter of his healing others of all sorts of sickness. It is true that he healed the blind, the sick, and the lame and even raised the dead.

They were earthly forms that did not know that such power was available to them, every one. Christ would raise his vibration to that of my love, then raise the one being prepared for healing. "When the form and the Christ and my Spirit," saith the Lord thy God, "are all one, then the healing will be complete, instant, and permanent." He was not using an unusual power for the true spiritual man; however, he was using a power that is truly unavailable for the physical man, or the form I call the shadow of the real.

The earthly man called his acts of love "healing miracles," and so they were for all the men of the earth. The spirit man knows the acts of Christ to be the power of the spirit being used in its natural and full way. The spirit man does not call these same deeds miracles; they are to his knowing the result of my spiritual love vibration of the one being healed.

In the days ahead, you will see much healing taking place the world over. There will be many who will do deeds that will make men think they are of me. If what they do is not borne of my love, then their healings are not mine as well.

Every healing that is of me will be one proclaimed by the Spirit and moved by my love. Spiritual man will heal physical man, and I will be pleased for man to once again use the power that I have given him from the beginning.

This lesson is for the knowing of all men.

LESSON 20

SPIRITUAL BLESSINGS AND PEACE

The words I am about to speak will divide the earthly man from the spirit man with a division so wide they shall never be confused again by one who reads these words.

You have many times used the right words with a meaning that has no truth in it at all. You give out your blessings as if they were like flakes of falling snow, not knowing that they are melted the instant they are touched by the warmth of the human hand. A true spiritual blessing is like the avalanche that breaks at mountaintop the moment the word of blessing is given, and it thunders down upon the recipient, and he is lost and covered over by the power and impact of the spiritual blessing given. If the best of the physical blessing is like one flake of fallen snow, quickly vanishing at the touch, and the very least of a spiritual blessing is like the avalanche from the mountain's downpouring, would you say with me the two blessings are seen as but one blessing in reality, though two were given forth?

The Spiritual Quest

The spirit can bless for blessing is a spiritual matter. There has never been a physical blessing for the unreal is not able to give forth anything other than what it has within itself.

Peace, like blessing, is a matter of the spirit and has never been the offering of the physical man.

National leaders proclaim we are once again at peace. They have been saying this for centuries, and we have found their words are but the sound of quiet between wars. I have never said that peace is the absence of war, yet is that not what man means when he declares his nation to be at peace?

"As long as we are not fighting against men of other lands, we are at peace." Is not this accepted to be the truth by men? I have not said it is the truth! I say unto you, my children of much love-giving, that the words of man are as temporal as he himself is.

The peace of the physical man is like words of much mouthing that break the still of silence, when silence is the very sound that is sought by the peacemakers themselves.

The peace of the spiritual man is a condition that is within, and from this place of knowing, there is never a sound that is brought forth.

Peace is not then the quiet of night when the sounds of war have ceased, nor is it the declaration of man's lips that we are at peace and all is well.

What, then, is this peace that is substance to the spirit and is without substance to the physical?

O Lord, I am searching for your answer for it has eluded man so long.

It has not eluded man at all! For when man turned from being the spiritual reality in control of this planet called earth, he gave up ever having peace until he returns and makes his claim of spiritual reality. Peace is spiritual and is unknown to the physical world.

Peace is the sound that is given off by the harmony of love and joy declared by the true spirit of my making and giving. I have told you what joy is, and I have told you what love is, and when the vibrations of these two are sounded together like the striking of two notes that blend in harmony, a third and new sound is given forth which is the sum of each of the two that were sounded forth. It is, however, a new sound or vibration that cannot be made by either of the other two alone.

Spirit man can be filled with joy and give it forth unto every man, and those around him will know the projection of the joy. The spiritual man can give forth my love to all around him, and men will surely know that they are being loved. Each of these is of great value when given, and the giving forth of them is important, like the very having of them is important, to the spiritual man.

When man gives them both forth, his love and his joy, he sets up a new vibration within his own body, mind or soul, and spirit, and this vibration of harmony of love and joy is known unto the giver as peace within. It is real. It has substance for the spirit man.

Do you now see clearly that it is not in just the having of these two, but the giving of these that makes the spirit man of their giving to be at peace? If you were filled with my love and did not give it forth, you would not be at peace within. It does not then come from the having alone of love and joy, but by giving does my peace come to the one who so gives of me. Can you see that it is for the spiritual man and not for the man of the flesh? The fleshly man has given his control to the unreal, and thus, the vibrations set up within his being are false, and he will never know peace. Does he not say we are at peace, only to go forth into the streets against his own family? It has been this way for the physical man since the day of his turning, Can you now see the spiritual peace of which I speak has no need of words, and we are as far from the earthly man's understanding of it as is the measure of his rebellion from me?

Now, finally, let me give you the clear understanding of my meaning of spiritual blessings. I have told you that physical man cannot give a spiritual blessing, and the two are like the snowflake and the avalanche when you try to compare the physical to the spiritual. The physical man says bless, and he means what he says, only there is little or no force behind his saying. To truly bless or to give a spiritual blessing is to extend the love of the Creator directly to the request of your spirit. The spiritual man says, "I extend to you the reality and presence of the living God, and may every need of harmony in your spirit be extended by God to you because of my bless-giving." Have I not said that when the spirit requests of me, the request is known and answered even before you can release the words into the ether?

Know this as well: Once the blessing is given, it must find a receptive place to do its work of harmony and healing. If the one to whom the blessing is extended does not accept with open spirit, then the blessing will not force its way upon the one in need.

"A blessing, once given, must have a receiver, for this is true of the very

Spiritual Blessings and Peace

nature of giving. The blessing will return to the giver if it is not accepted with open spirit, and thus, the blessing will find a place of reception. It could not have gone forth at all if the giver had not been in the proper spirit before calling upon me," saith the Lord thy God.

I am God and the Giver of all that is good. When one blesses another, it extends the spirit of my abundant love to new centers of being.

Give forth the blessings of God often, and direct them to children of my creation who stand receptive and in need. Soon the world will be a place where my children are abundantly blessed, and your very eyes will behold the wonders that are for the people who so live and work with me.

Bless you, my sons and daughters. For as I give you a blessing, you are truly blessed, and even now you know within you that you have surely received of me, for I am thy God and the Giver of all that is good.

This lesson has just begun with this ending.

The Spiritual Quest

LESSON 21

THE CENTER OF MAN

When I speak, I speak of the spiritual and not of the physical; thus, the center of which I speak cannot be found by the hand of the skilled surgeon nor by the point of any blade. If this were not so, then man would quickly speak as to what was found at man's center, and the subject would be closed. Some men speak of the mind, or soul, and they can give us many volumes of great detail about the inner workings of man's mind. When you have gone to the center of man's mind, or soul, you have not begun to deal with the matter of this lesson.

"Write," saith the Lord God of all men. I shall now speak of the true center of man and what he shall find there. True man is the spirit man of my creation, and I have given him all the power to do the deeds of a loving son. The power of which I speak is generated from this center of man. Yet from this same center, you will find the point where all is still for there can be no formation of spiritual activity without the stillness of the center. In this very same center, you will find the seed of full change that has been planted by my Spirit, whom man knows as the Holy Spirit.

It is this seed, which is planted by the Holy Spirit, that, when nurtured, will grow until the spiritual man and all of his powers will have transferred these powers into the full activity of the form. In this condition, the spirit of man is in control, and the form, which I call the shadow, can be called upon by the spirit to act according to the spiritual directions. Then the full change takes place where the spirit, or the real, and the form have become one, and my true sonship or daughtership is known to completion in that son or daughter of my greatest handiwork.

When the apostle Paul said, "Not I, but Christ who dwells within me," he spoke of the full and true change that had been affected within his physical being when it had been given over to the spirit. When man speaks of the Christ, he speaks of the full range that took place in Jesus of Nazareth. The full man, Jesus of Nazareth, and the full God Spirit, Christ, had become one.

Perfection is found at the center of the spiritual man. Did not my Son the Christ say unto you, "Be ye perfect even as your Father in heaven is perfect"? What he was saying to all those around him and to all men down though the ages was that the spiritual center of spiritual man is perfection. When the physical has given full control over to the spiritual self and the oneness is complete, then the perfection, which is known to be the center of the spirit man, becomes the control center for the physical man. He is then perfected as was the Christ.

When man says all these things are beyond him, he speaks the truth for all of these matters are of the spirit and are truly beyond the physical man. When the spirit man speaks, he will speak from knowing and will say, "All of these spiritual realities are to be found in the center of me."

The Center of Man

You ask, "How can a place of such guilt be a place of such great power and activity?"

The activity of the spirit and the activity of the form are not at all the same. The spirit causes great accomplishments to come forth from the activity known as quiet rest. However, since it has no true power within it, the form moves about with a great deal of activity and, in reality, accomplishes nothing of eternal value. Power of spirit comes from the center of this rest, while the power of the flesh is nothing more than the active using up of what little there is to it and giving it the name of great accomplishment.

The center of man is the place where my Spirit dwells. I speak of my temple. Would you suppose that a spirit (for I am God and I am spirit) would find need of a form and would call it a temple? I am spirit, and the manifestation of my Spirit is the form. The form is not on the earth plane to control, but to give control to the real, which is spirit of my Spirit. The form allows the joy and love of the spirit to be expressed on the earth plane of my creation. Every child on this earth was made as my temple in which I choose to dwell. I cannot dwell in a form who says, "I am in control," and denies the spirit for then the form claims to be the real, and there is no truth in the claim. I cannot dwell in a false form that claims to be the real.

The form, then, is an empty temple and is still far less than all of its claims. There is, therefore, true value at the center of man, for the man of my speaking is spirit, and I am truth, and I am value, and I am to be found at the center of the spiritual man. Yes, I have said it, and it is the truth. I am the Lord thy God, and I am at the center of the real, the true, the spirit man. What do you find at the center of man? Nothing! Nothing when the man of our speaking is but the form of the real. What do you find at the center of man? God! God and all of his stillness and power when you speak of the spiritual man.

You cannot change the truth of these words any more than you can change the reality of your spirit. What you the earthly man can do is give up your hold on the unreal form and allow your true and spiritual self to take charge of the form. Then, and only then, will you come to know the true center of your being is the place where I am to be found.

Thus saith the Lord God of all men.

This lesson brings to a close the third series of seven. We have shared much, my son, and yet there is so much more awaiting my spiritual children who, in faith and love, do come unto me.

The Spiritual Quest

Series Four

IV

The Spiritual Quest

LESSON 22

THE INWARD JOURNEY

Write.

All that we have spoken of thus far is of no value unless the matter that is before us becomes the true quest of every man and woman. Man has developed tools to take him to the heart of the earth. He has climbed over the face of it and sailed all of her seas. He has ridden upon rockets and scratched the surface of space, but there is one trip before him that is more important to him than all he has done thus far. All of these things were done by the shadow of the real and carry with them, even in their accomplishment, the limitation of the earthly man.

The journey I am prepared to describe for you is one that can only be taken by the spiritual man. Therefore, none of his present standard of tools is usable for this journey. There are conditions, however, that must be met before this inward journey can begin. It is not based upon any of the expected tools that man would think necessary for this spiritual undertaking. In fact, it is based more upon what man does not use, for his earthly choosings are limitations to the spirit.

The Spiritual Quest

Let me begin by saying nothing that you have by the way of things is necessary. You will not employ matters of your mind or intellect for they quickly become burdens rather than true spiritual helps. This is a spiritual journey, and only the true and real man will make this journey. "The true man is spirit, and it is his spirit that shall move to the place where I am to be found," saith the Lord thy God. The vehicle of your moving is the true desire of your spirit to go to the very center of your being. Do not look down at your body and think you are going to the center of what you can see. I say unto you, "You are going to the center of what you are."

Every man and woman was made first spirit of my Spirit, and then the form of the real was manifested in what you know as the body. I spoke of what you are even before the body of what you see existed at all. If you are willing to go within, then the first act is of your own doing. No man can start another upon this glorious spiritual trip within. The strength of your desire will determine the speed with which you move within. "Can it be in a moment?" you ask of me, and I will answer, "It can be if you will it to be, and then know that your will shall have full expression." I have said will and knowing. The act of the will is first yours, and so everything begins the moment you will it to begin. The knowing of which I speak is spiritual knowing, and the very presence of knowing will indicate to you the journey has begun.

"Knowing is a spiritual sense that begins the moment one has turned away from the matters of the earthly form and unto the matter of the spirit," saith the Lord thy God. Truly, just in the turning from earthly unto the spirit will all be made available unto every man and woman of my love. "Why then, if it is so simple, do not all turn unto me," you ask.

The Inward Journey

Because in the state of rebellion, man believes I am far from him or would not receive him even as he is, and so it is his own sin and rebellion that keep him from me. If you doubt these words are of me, you have but to truly turn in spirit unto me, and all I have said will come to pass within you. "There is no pretending in the matter. You either keep control and, thus, keep your back turned upon me, or you give your spirit control and turn unto me," saith the Lord thy God, who may be found at the end of your inward journey.

"How do I begin?" you ask.

Stop all activity, and get away from all sounds or any matter that requires the use of your senses for they are distractions to your spirit. Let your spirit speak unto me, and you may say, "Lord God of this universe, as your son or daughter, I have wondered far from your spirit, and I have rebelled against you, but I stand before you now truly ready to return unto you." If these words come from your mouth or your mind, be assured you will not hear from me, and the trip that you are about to make will be no more than an exercise of the mind. If, however, these words come from your spirit unto me, you may be assured you will clearly hear from me these words: "Come unto me, my son or daughter of my great love, for your heavenly Father awaits you." There will be a quickening of your spirit, and because of your sense of knowing which can only be employed by the spirit of man, it will also give you the assurance that your trip is real. You then have but to continue, and with every step you take in the spirit, you will hear and know you are coming unto me.

You ask, "How long does the inward journey take, and when does it end?"

It takes as long as you choose to move in your spirit, and it ends when your own knowing of the spirit tells you. It can also end by calling these truths foolish, and you turn away from me and go back into your old ways.

When you look at your old ways and know that they are not for you, it is a sign of the spirit that the change has begun, and the spiritual journey within is real unto you. If you have to ask, "Is it over?", you may be assured it is not, for as long as you do not know the ending of the journey, you may be assured it is continuing still.

There is great joy and love expressed along the inward way, and you will know a peace as you give out the joy and love you have found to another. These are but signs along the way to add to your knowing that this journey is real to your spirit and not a game played upon you by your own mind. Your own sense of being will begin to express itself within you, and truly others around you will confirm from without what you know to be taking place from within. The sense of life and its richer and true values become apparent to you, and the love that is of me becomes a part of the true you. It is not an effort on your part; it is just there and is a true joy of your spirit. The sense of the universal allows your spirit to reach out into all surrounding realms, and you begin to know that you have new values within and without.

The true, spiritual you has begun to emerge, and the false, earthly shadow that has controlled you in the past is losing its hold upon you. It becomes a joy for you to speak of your God and Creator, and I say it is also a joy for me to see you in this condition for it means another one of my children is returning unto me. You will now find no value in the old, and true value in matters of the spirit will be yours to hold and to make a part of your own spiritual being.

There will be a spiritual awareness of light as you approach the center, for you will find light, stillness, all power, all love, and a full sense of all that is within you. You will at your journey's end find me, the Lord God of your making, and you will know because of the encounter. And then to you, there will be a burst of such love, peace, joy, and all that I am within you that the very center of you will ring forth with the truth, "The Lord God lives and he is within me!" These will be the truths that burst across your knowing! The body and the mind, or soul, will have nothing to offer you, for all that is of true value will be yours. You will not ask, "Is the inward journey over?" You will know! And in knowing, there will be a thrill that cannot be offered by the sailing of the seas or the climbing of mountain tops. Not even the journey into space can compare with the one that you have taken to find yourself in the presence of the living God!

You will also have to your knowing the truth that with the ending of the inward journey, which was one made by your spirit alone, the outward journey is now ready to begin. This you will not make alone for I will walk with you every step of the way, and it will be full of new joys, truths, and love, and you will know the presence of the Lord thy God.

The inward journey ends, so the outward may begin.

The Spiritual Quest

LESSON 23

THE OUTWARD JOURNEY

Let us move forward in your knowing, for the encounter at the end of the inward journey is one that is to be made by every child of my making. For when the inward journey is complete, there is such joy over the encounter that my children are content to remain in that condition with no offer to make the outward journey.

Let me clearly say that when the inward and the outward journeys are over, then the vessel is clean and ready for the filling of the Holy Spirit of my Spirit. Have I not clearly said that he would come and work with you on all matters of the spirit? This was a deep truth spoken by my Son the Christ, and the filling is planned for every man and woman of this earth. Is it now clear that the inward journey of man's spirit unto God and the outward journey with God are but two parts of the total plan?

The filling of the Holy Spirit is to prepare you for the seed of spiritual planting within you, and the seed will grow till the full spirit of my making of you will be seen and the old will be gone. Behold, all things become new.

The Spiritual Quest

The apostle Paul said, "For me to live is Christ." He also said, "It is not I who live, but Christ who liveth within me." That was not a condition prepared just for Paul, nor just for you who read these words.

The fruit of your spiritual tree will grow unto the fullness thereof, and when you begin your fruit-giving, you will then be the full child of my spiritual making. You will know the great power of my love, and you will do the acts of the spirit that will help raise your fellow men unto a clearer knowing of the Lord God and of all that is real for every man.

With this clearly before you, now do you see the great value in the outward journey that we shall make together? "I have explained the matters that are to follow so you may understand the truly great importance that must be placed upon the outward journey. It is one that is made between the spirit of the man or woman and my Spirit," saith the Lord God.

I have called this our garden walk, for all matters of new awareness and joy are yours to behold as we make this walk together. It is one of great quiet and solitude between us. You will enjoy the moments we are together, and it will be a time of instruction from my Spirit unto your spirit.

It is proper for you to ask, "How will I know that the words that come clearly to my spirit and then into my mind are from God and not out of the deeper recesses of my own mind?" My ways are always above those of your own, but in this walk, we will be close, spirit to spirit, and the words that I speak to you can be tested in several ways.

You will always find that my words to your spirit will be in harmony with the words of my Scriptures. My words unto you will be matters of the spirit and will have the support of eternal truth that have come to man through the ages. When you share these matters with another spirit-filled person, you will find an affirmative response in them that will come forth quickly and boldly. A person who has no spiritual knowing will hear the truths spoken by my Spirit, but will not be able to confirm anything that comes from me. I speak the truth, and it needs not the defense of man for it to stand the test of anyone who wishes to fight against it.

You will also find in the outward walk that when questions of the spirit come before you, the true answers that are needed will be before you as well. They are there for your use, for then we will walk together again spirit by spirit. You will also note that you meet your daily tasks with new vigor, and you now have solutions where before only the questions were clearly seen.

There will be the testimony of others, even from some you do not know, for they will declare the changes in you that have become apparent to their spirits. If you encounter one that belongs to the forces of darkness, there will be great resistance, and you will notice it without your having to speak even one word. Your physical rest will be more complete, and you will deal with every problem that faces you with new vigor, and you cannot know failure for this walk is one of the spirit and there is naught but success as we make this spiritual trip together. Your spirit will know my presence, and there will be a great peace and assurance within you that cannot be explained away by logical words of man. Your views on matters of the past will have a great, new clarity, and you will make your decisions with a great assurance that the results will be pleasing to both of our spirits. I have called this walk the garden walk, for you will look upon life with a new freshness, and there will be many questions of the spirit that you will ask and have answers waiting for you before the question is complete. You will have a new joy in the reading and study of my Word, for I will now feed and nourish your spirit, and you will be aware of daily growth.

You will not need the confirmation of those around you for you to continue this outward journey, but you will be pleased to know that others around you can see or sense a part of the change that is going on within you. There will be a clear knowing.

If one you dearly love comes up behind you and speaks, you would not even need to turn around to know who it is that stands in your presence. Likewise, from the encounter with me, you will know my voice and the presence of my Spirit, and when I speak, you will not need the confirmation of anyone to agree with your spiritual knowing.

As much as a joy this spiritual journey is, it must end in this form for the filling of the Holy Spirit which is to follow. You must know now that I shall never depart from you, and our spirits will finally blend into a full and final oneness. There can be no separation at that great place of filling. This is a part of the preparation that will make of you a great and useful vessel of my love-filling. I look with pleasure upon our walk for it pleases me to share the things I had planned for you from the beginning of my creation.

This lesson ends, but there are great new spiritual fields for us to explore together in your time of great growing.

This lesson ends, but now it must be clear to you that there is much more for us to do spirit to spirit together.

The Spiritual Quest

LESSON 24

THE EARTHLY MAN BECOMES THE SPIRITUAL SON

Write.

Let us begin with the facts of the spirit man. I am the Lord God of all men, and I am spirit, for I am real, and spirit is all there is to the real of my giving. I made man in my image, and man was and is spirit. It is the spirit of man that is real and eternal. At this point, there was nothing yet in form on earth, and there was no physical man to be seen walking upon the earth. Then the real spirit sent a manifest form of the real, and the form is held together by the real spirit of man which is of me and my giving.

Now upon the earth, there is a body to be seen by the eyes of the earth. There is a spirit at the very center of this form, and the real and the true spirit remains with me, the Creator and Giver of all that is good. You then have upon the earth a spirit-filled and spirit-controlled form that is not the real, but only the manifestation of the real. You have my sons and daughters who walk upon the earth and know me and know my voice, for they are form controlled by the spirit. They are filled with my love and power, and all that I am is for them to be and use at the will of the spirit. All that I have made is good, and man and woman are the joy of my creation.

Man has turned from my love and all-giving and no longer walks in the path of my choosing.

Know ye this now: The spirit of man is still with me for I am spirit and I am life, and if the spirit were to leave me, it would be no more. If the spirit of man were no longer a reality, there would be nothing to hold the form of man together, and therefore, the form would be no more as well. It is not the form that maintains the spirit, but the spirit that maintains the form. There is reality in the spirit and none in the form.

Do you now see with your spiritual eyes the words I speak are the truth for all men to hear and understand? I would not take away my love from you because of your rebellion, but in your rebellion, you gave up most of the power that was yours when you walked as the spirit being of my Spirit.

I did not take away your power, for the spirit that you are has all of the gifts that were given out of my great love for you. Notice, I did not say your spirit had, but has all of the gifts of my love. At the very moment you read these words, I tell you, all that you once were and had awaits you upon your return.

The return that I speak of is not from one place to another, but is a condition of change that must take place before all of the truths that I have spoken are yours through your own spiritual knowing. As I have said, they have always been yours and are yours even now, but until your spiritual knowing has replaced your physical sensing, to you they are as if I had never given nor spoken them unto you. You are a spirit with all of my gifts available unto you. Your form you call the body is not the real and, therefore, has none of the gifts for they are for the spirit only.

Because I have placed my Spirit at the center of every form man, man has from time to time used a portion of his power. It was always as free or as limited as his knowing in the spirit. I have said that man cannot hold knowing in part. "If man has spiritual knowing, then for that time he has given his control once again to the real, and the form acts as it is guided by the spirit. It does not do anything that is not directed by the spirit for if it does, you may be assured the form man is in control and the spirit must wait in love and patience for the form of the real to end its false rule so the real of man can once again know and share the joy of my presence," saith the Lord thy God.

Man of the form will say, "Nonsense," to these words, and he speaks the truth, for to the form, the words of the spirit are a "non-sense," and he will continue to walk in his darkness that has no light in it at all. Man of the spirit will say it is the truth, for he does not use his earthly sensing at all, but employs his spiritual knowing, and to this one, truth is indeed truth. You are my children. You are spirit of my Spirit. You have but to turn unto me and, thus, take the control of your being from the form and give it unto the spirit.

It was man who turned from God, and it will be man who will turn unto God. "With your back unto me, the form rules, and you have nothing but shadows, for I am the light that giveth the shadow that you now call real. With your face unto me, you are light of the true light, and the real spirit, which you are, once again walks in me and I in you," saith the God of light and love.

You ask, "When do I turn?" Now is the day of your return and your glory.

You ask, "How is this done?" Know that I speak to you the truth of the ages, and you give the spirit, which is the real, control.

You ask, "How do I give the spirit control?" You are spirit; know this and hold not on to what you sense, and you will have in its place the assurance of my Word. You will know, and knowing is of the spirit, not of the form.

I ask you, "Is it from darkness unto light that gives evidence that you have turned?" A man or woman whose form controls and whose spirit awaits cannot cry out his or her agreement with the truth of this lesson. A man or woman whose spirit controls and whose form awaits its instructions can do nothing but cry out his or her agreement with the truth of my Spirit.

Come, for my truth, love, and power await the spirit man of my making.

LESSON 25

TO KNOW EVEN AS YOU ARE KNOWN

Write, for these words will quicken the spirits of all who are open to the truth they will find herein.

There have always been men who accepted the truth that the Lord God of all creation is all knowing. It has been used of man in many ways to avoid the truth of his own relationship to that all-knowing Spirit of his Creator.

Man often says, "God knows everything," and he uses it as a comfort to his own position of knowing very little. Man has then separated the knowing of God and his own knowing, which is again used as a protection from taking his true responsibility. As long as the Lord God knows all and man knows individually very little, then man says he cannot be blamed for the difficulties that he gets into because of his self-appointed lacking.

"The knowing of my Spirit," saith the Lord thy God, "and the knowing of the man of the form are not even the same in the choice of words." Man says knowing is knowing, and I say they are not the same at all. When man speaks of his knowing, he is referring to a level of mind and intellect that is based upon the accumulated facts of the centuries. I tell you now that all the facts of knowing of the form man, which I call the shadow of the real, are not facts at all. They are based on physical reason, logic, and every other form of man-made fact. There are some facts that are held by man, but they come by the way of his spirit, not his intellect. When the premise or the foundation upon which man builds his structure is the knowing of the mind, then they are as false as the man himself. (I am aware that these words seem harsh and even frightening to the one who gives this matter his full attention.)

One day, the spirit man will be in position to bring my truth before man, and the truth of my Spirit will cause most of what man now holds to be set aside, for the real will always replace the unreal. Physical man himself is not even real, that is, not real until his spirit is in charge of his form. Do you see that since the man of the earth is but the shadow of the real, all of the so-called "facts" that are so based on the assumption of the shadow man are like he is, only shadows of the real truth for every man? I am spirit, and when I speak of knowing, I speak of things the way they are, not the way they seem to be.

The real problem began when man of the spirit turned from me and gave control over to the shadow of the real, which you call the earthly man. In his turning, he gave up the five key spiritual senses [see Lesson 40, the ninth through the thirteenth senses] that are far beyond those he now employs. Man lost his sense of knowing, for the spirit man is not based on any of the unreal tools called real by the shadow man. The sense of knowing is a part of the spiritual range that, when employed properly and fully, will enable the spiritual man, who has a manifested form, to do deeds that are natural for him and will be called supernatural by the shadow man.

There will be new science and math employed by the spirit man based on knowing fact rather than on facts of the mind. For to know in the spirit is to know things as they are in reality. To know in the shadow is to know things as they seem to be. To tell man he can travel by new methods without the use of any known vehicle is a truth of the spirit, and that way is available to the spirit man. To give these words to the shadow man is to give him cause to say it is not true; these words to him are unreal. Do you see? The real to the shadow man is called unreal, and the truly unreal is called real by him.

When man turned from me, he set his face upon a false world and put his back to the only true and real that was ever before him. Man has but four senses to my knowing, for I gave him taste and smell as one called the sense of refreshment. He employs hearing, sight, and touch, and here in this very narrow, self-limiting range, man has been content to use them as the basis for his knowing structure. Can you see that sensing of the flesh and knowing of the spirit are not the same at all, and the same word should not even be employed to describe what man calls knowing?

"Time, space, and the structure of the elements, as well as the universe, were based upon a different set of facts from my knowing," saith the Lord thy God, "than from the sensing of limited man." I know you each and every one as you are, not as you seem to be. When you return once again to the spiritual reality that you are and have always been in my making, then you will, as you grow in spirit, be able to employ for your spiritual use the spiritual senses, one of which is knowing. Thus, I declare unto you that man of the spirit will know even as he is known. You will use fully and properly all of the new ranges open to you, and you will deal with the sense of the universal in your knowing. Man of the flesh looks up to the heavens and wonders about all he sees, or senses with his eyes. Man of the spirit looks up into the heavens and knows about all that he cannot see or sense at all.

Man of the earth will use his senses to tell him the answers to the questions of his heart, and they will be as limited as the one from which the answers came. Man of the spirit will use his sense of knowing and will have no need to even question for the answers needed are already a part of his knowing. The spirit man will then know even as he is known.

The lesson has ended only to begin again with you when you wish to truly know.

LESSON 26

STRIVING AFTER GOD

"Write, my son, for the flow of my Spirit within you allows these words to come forth of me," saith the Lord thy God.

Let me clearly and quickly separate the spiritual striving after me from the physical attempts to reach me. When the physical man, or shadow of the real, strives after me, it only brings exhaustion and frustration for there is nothing of the physical realm that can enter the spiritual kingdom. You know it to be true: When the physical man leaves the earth plane, all of his possessions belong to others that remain behind. Is this not true to your knowing?

With this so clearly before you, why does man persist in trying to bring the earthly things over into the world of the real that you now know to be the spiritual? Because man still calls real these earthly things that have no reality in them at all! Man hears of a new group that has gathered with claims of great power and truth, so quickly he goes to this gathering and sits at the feet of children as they unveil their new discovery. He is then given volumes of things to do, to read, to wear, to make, all of which are supposed to help him find the strivings of his mind and body.

"These things are full of great activity, but there is no spirit in them. For if they were of me," saith the Lord thy God, "then they would cease their great activity and direct their spirits unto me."

"Where is the place for the finding of you, Lord God?" your spirit cries out, and I say unto you, "The very place where you now stand." There is nowhere to go but within, for in my Word I have told you the Spirit of God dwells within. I have placed the spark of my being in every child of my creation. Notice that I have said unto you, "The spirit cries out unto me, whereas before the cries that were found in his quest were matters of the body and the mind, or soul, of man."

I have called these lessons *The Spiritual Quest* for I am spirit and I am the Lord thy God, and man must strive after me in spirit and in truth, and then he will surely find me. I have not been hiding from man, nor have I tried to make the way of his finding more difficult for him. I am spirit, and the path of the Holy Spirit is not attainable by searching with the body or the mind of man. When you rebelled and turned from me, you got off of the spiritual path that we were walking together, and you made new paths of your own. You called them good, and you called them beautiful, and they were to you exactly according to your calling. "They were not the paths of the Spirit, and they were not called beautiful by my Spirit," saith the Lord thy God.

For centuries, man has wandered his own paths, and each time he makes a new one, it becomes less clear and has less grandeur, yet man calls it "beautiful," and so it is to his calling. Man says, "I'm striving after

God," and so he gives new names to old foolish findings that have been found and discarded by another before him. Man has lifted his hands in praise to the sun that gives him light, and though it was made by me for the use of all men, it is a striving of the mind and not of the spirit.

Man comes upon the great pyramids of an ancient culture, and he finds new forms of math and science that are beyond his knowing, and so he strives to find all the answers that these ancient people had. I tell you that when he has found all that they knew, still his striving will not be over; it will have just begun, for only the spiritual striving will bring man back unto his Creator. It is there all the answers are truly found. I tell you now a truth of the spirit that is still a mystery unto the earthly man. Man is still asking how the stones of the great pyramids were placed one upon the other. I tell you that the man of my Spirit cannot only place the stones one upon the other, but if it were a matter of spiritual need, he could cause the very stones to appear where there were none to behold but moments before.

I say unto you once again that the spiritual man of my making shall have all that is of me when he is fully once again mine. If I could make an earth and place my spiritual children upon it, could not my children when they are full spirit do all that I have done? I am your Lord God and father-mother of every child of my Spirit who is found upon this earthly plane. What I have in store for those who strive in spirit after me, the words or ways of the earthly shadow of man cannot contain nor comprehend.

"What must I do to find you?" says the man of the form and mind. "Nothing," is my reply for neither the form nor the mind can find me. I am not to be found by even the best of the unreal.

"What must I do to find you?" says the spirit man who is striving after me.

"Come unto me, for you are once again on the path of my making," saith the Lord thy God.

"What must I do," says the earthly striver, "to get upon the path of the Lord?"

Know that I am spirit, and give up all of your earthly exercises of body and mind striving. Then know that you are spirit of my Spirit. If you say, "I cannot now say I know I am spirit," then accept it to be true and come unto me, for as man of the spirit comes unto me, his knowing begins and grows with his every step.

"Can man move to full knowing all at once?" you ask.

He can, and may, if he wills it to be. I now speak of the matters of the spirit, and there is no limitation in the spirit. Let your striving be constant, and do not look back upon your old ways, for the spirit that strives after me and then walks the old path of darkness will find it darker than ever before. Know this: You cannot walk both the path of physical striving and the path of spiritual striving as well. Nor can you go from one to the other and back again, for only one path of striving is real, and that is the path of the spirit. Man has called the physical world around him real for so long that he has placed it in his knowing and lost his true and only way. "Strive in spirit after the Lord thy God, and you will find me within and waiting. Strive in body and mind after anything of your choosing, and you will not find me, but only the very shadow of

Striving After God

your own foolish self will you find," saith the Lord thy God. If you choose to strive at all, why not strive after the real and the eternal and that which will allow you to know in fullness the Lord thy God?

The lesson ends with a call unto your spirit.

The Spiritual Quest

LESSON 27

OVERFLOWING JOY

Write, for these words are a thrill to the spirit of everyone who taketh these words to heart.

I have shared with you the meaning of joy as it is expressed in an earthen vessel we call the form of man. Joy is a spiritual gift from my creative hand of giving, and so the gift is given of my Spirit and received by the spirit of man. It is then a transfer from spirit unto spirit, but it has a manifestation in the earthly form of the real. You should clearly understand then that all of the usual matters called joy by the men of the earth are as far from the reality of spiritual joy as the form of the real, called the earthly man, is from the spiritual reality of that same man.

Man says, "There is joy in victory."

I say, "There can be joy in defeat, if through that defeat man has come to the encounter of the living God and has received the joy of the Creator in that encounter."

Man says, "There is great joy when much wealth is received."

The Spiritual Quest

I say unto you, "You have nothing if you gain the ownership of the earth and all that is in it and have not found me, thy God, the Maker of all your earthly holdings."

I tell you, "There is no joy in all of the earth's vast wealth."

Now I declare unto you that man shall not take the vow of poverty in order to be pleasing unto me and receive the joy of my giving. We are dealing in a spiritual matter, and it is the spiritual encounter and acceptance of any giving that transfer the joy of my Spirit unto the spirit of man. If through poverty man comes to the place where he will turn unto me, then for that one, the poverty has been a spiritual blessing, and his earthly loss cannot be compared to his spiritual gain of great joy.

Let it be clearly understood that the spirit-filled man who walks with me and uses his great wealth to turn other men from their way of folly unto their Creator is a great blessing to every man. He will have much joy as an outgrowth of the wealth that he possesses.

Man expresses a joy around certain earthly company he keeps, and to his limited knowing of the meaning of joy, to him it is joy. I say unto you, "If you experienced at once all the joys that are listed by the true earthly man and then without notice or warning experienced the true joy of the spirit, it would be unto you as if the joys of man did not exist." This is a truth, for what man calls joy are unreal expressions of the form of the real man. Since there is no reality in the form man, then there can be no reality in what he knows to be his joy. When that same man becomes the man of the spirit, or a real man in an earthly form, then the joy of his knowing and expression will be the joy of my Spirit, and he will be joyful indeed. The joy of the earth is but the shadow of the real and truly has nothing of its own that will last beyond the moment of its apparent presence. The joy of the spirit is as eternal as the Creator and the Giver of it, and therefore, it is found to remain and even grow as the spiritual growth of the individual takes place.

I have called this lesson "Overflowing Joy," and thus far, we have seen what it is not, as well as what it is, and how man receives it.

I would now speak to the matter of its overflowing. I have said the joy in the spirit man is real, for he is real and, thus, can contain its reality. Can the shadow of the pan hold any of the water if you try to fill it, or would all of the water be lost and wasted? Can you now see the earthly form of man, which I know to be the shadow of the real, cannot receive the joy of my giving for it, too, would be lost and wasted upon such a one? Joy of the spirit is given unto the spirit of man, and thus, it is held. As the spirit man grows more and more in his spirit and less and less of a shadow of the real, my joy is ever filling as he is ever growing.

Again I ask you, "Can the thimble of the woman's sewing hold the refreshment of the drinking pail that is found by the well?"

"No," you would quickly answer, "if all of the water of the pail were poured into the thimble, there would be a great overflowing upon the ground, but in the end, the thimble would hold no more than its original fitting for the woman's finger." That, too, is a kind of overflowing, but one that is wasteful and not very useful. Let me speak of the spirit man who grows day by day and, as he grows, is filled full of joy. He continues his growth until he is the full spirit man of my making and he is filled with the joy of my Spirit. Still there has not been an overflowing, only a filling, but now the true and full spirit man is ready for what I call the spiritual overflowing.

When the container is as large as I have made it to be and it is as full of my joy as was given of me, then as I give more of my joy, that spirit one of me gives unto others all that is his to give. He gives from the overflow, but gives all that is within him. Do you now see that only the full spiritual container is ready to give all that he is and has, and only in all giving can there be true overflow of my Spirit unto all men? If I made of you a gallon container and began the spiritual flow of my Spirit unto you, would not soon all that you first received be given forth, and the gallon you now contain would not be the same one of your first filling? Water that does not flow soon becomes unusable, and if only the water of the top overflow were given off to others, soon the water that filled the container would not be of use at all. Only the full spiritual one is willing to give all that is within him, and only in this way can the true meaning of spiritual joy to overflowing come to the light of all men.

There are partially filled men who say, "I shall give ten percent of all that I have, and God will surely bless." I will bless even the smallest gift and the giver that have truly in spirit given unto me, but how can I give my full measure of joy to one who is but ten percent of a container of my spiritual making?

There are some who say, "Fifty percent of all that I have and am goes to God." This is better, but it is not enough.

A very few say, "Then ninety percent will go to God, and I shall keep only ten percent for myself." This is better still, but the plan of my joy filling to overflowing is not yet complete.

"When the shadow man is gone and the spirit man stands in reality where the shadow once stood, this child of my love says, 'All that I am shall be given,' and unto that one, I am able to give my all, even to overflowing," saith the Lord thy God.

This lesson is finished, and may your overflowing begin.

The Spiritual Quest

LESSON 28

SPIRITUAL ASKING OF THE LORD

I have made man free to choose. Spiritual man will make the right choice, for the basis of his choosing is in me. When the decision is made by man of the form, it will always be based upon limited truth, and the results will be as limited as the one who holds the responsibility of making the decision.

Your concern over my words to you about the election should be set aside at this time. I would not interfere with the wishes of the people of your land. They are all my children, and they are all free to do my will or that of their own. If the man so chosen by the people of the land will allow his spirit to take charge, then I can use him for great accomplishment in this land.

It was as much a responsibility on your part to send my words to him as it was a responsibility on his part to act upon the words received. He is only partially mine in our spirit-to-spirit walk, and I will use all of him that he will allow. I spoke to you of a loss that will bring his attention back unto me. When that occurs, I will then direct your attention

The Spiritual Quest

towards him. You will note that I said he will lead the people of this nation, and so it has come to pass as I have said.

I have said it many times in the words of my mouth you call Scripture that man can ask of me anything, and I will give according to his asking. I have said, "If you love me, ask; if you believe, ask; if you know, ask. Ask and it shall be given you; seek and ye shall find."

Man of the earth has used every excuse of his mind to say, "God does not really mean anything." He has twisted the matter of my will into a thousand new forms, each of which allows him to sidestep the truth of my Spirit.

"I will now say clearly, finally, and fully what it is that man must come to know if he wishes to ask of me," saith the Lord thy God and the Giver of every request. Let these words of truth now go forth unto every man.

Man of the flesh, the man I call the shadow of the real, can ask forever and will not receive a single gift of his asking. Do not confuse the matter by giving examples where earthly men have received gifts from me. I have said it clearly: The man of the form cannot ask of his heavenly Father and receive from me. The form man and the Spirit of God are not upon the same plane of reality, and I say unto you clearly that the spirit giveth unto the spirit, the form giveth unto the form, and they do not ask nor give one to the other. Hear me clearly, for I am not saying man cannot receive from God the gifts of his heart. I am saying the man who uses his form only to do the asking cannot receive from me.

Again I say that man of the spirit may ask of me and he will receive the gifts of his request even while he is asking. Have I not clearly said the man of my creation is spirit of my Spirit, and the earthly form you call body is but the manifested form of the real? Now do you see clearly that in each place of my Word where I spoke of asking, it was always conditioned by the spirit? God is love; is this not true?

Then when I say, "Love me and ask anything," do you understand the request comes from the spirit unto the Spirit? The sense of knowing is a spiritual sense and can only be used by one who has turned once again unto me. When the form man says unto the spirit, or the real man, "You are in control; use me as you will," then the requests of that one are to me a joy to be fulfilling to the fullest measure. You then have but to hold the request until the spiritual reality becomes manifest form.

It has always been a concern to some men that I would say, "Ask anything of me and thou shalt receive." I have always meant there to be no limitation upon the requests of the spirit man. How could a God of all gifts give, at any time, only a part of the spirit's request? To give but a part of any gift would make of me less than what I am, and that cannot be.

Do not concern yourself with the openness of my willingness to give any request. Would the spirit of my making ask of me any requests of a foolish nature? No, only the form of the real, because of a limited knowing, makes requests of the nature of itself. The form cannot receive; therefore, there is no basis for your concern. Does an all-giving spirit make a request of greed? No, for it cannot. Can a spirit of love request in any other form but in love?

Does an all-knowing spirit request of me that which he or she knows is beyond the spiritual law boundary of giving? Do you now see why the gifts of God are for all who might request of me? I speak of spiritual requests with spiritual gifts that are to follow. Let me remind you everyone that I have said, "Seek ye first my kingdom, which is found within every man and is spiritual in nature, and every other thing shall be added unto you." It is not my words that change for I speak in truth; man changes and comes to know, and then he may request anything, knowing it is his even before the asking.

You ask me, "Why are some able to ask and receive and hold the manifested form of that request far more quickly than others?"

The limitation is always with the man or woman doing the asking, not with me, the Giver. Each will be given according to his faith. This word *faith* that I have just used should be clearly understood by all spirits that seek after me. When the man of the flesh (or the form or the shadow of the real) speaks of faith, he is speaking of a belief based upon hope that the matter of the faith will come to him. It cannot for it is a spiritual law that the form cannot employ. Man often then says, "It was not God's will to give it," or "My faith was not strong enough to make it come to pass." These and all the rest of man's excuses are not valid. The truth is that as long as he is in control, the form man cannot receive the supply of the law of faith and spiritual giving. I say unto you, "It cannot come to pass."

When the real man of the spirit, of my Spirit, speaks of the word *faith*, he or she is applying the spiritual law: The spirit asks of me in knowing even though the form of faith has not yet been manifested, yet the knowing remains clear to the spirit who is asking of me. Then the request must come to pass. Therefore, the request, though not yet seen or manifested, remains real to the spirit, and therefore, the faith brings into form reality, which has already, and has always, been to the spirit a reality.

The problem has always been in the past that man has tried to deal with matters of the spirit with the use of the form alone. Let me also make it clear to the degree the faith request comes from the spirit, to that same degree will the manifestation be found.

When the spirit-controlled man says, "I know God will give me the gift of my asking," be assured the request of the spirit is given.

When the flesh-controlled man says, "I have faith that God will give me the gift of my asking," be assured the request of the flesh will not – yea, cannot – be given. Thus, he prepares his excuses and finds ways to place the blame on all around him. Tell this child of my deepest love what is required of him. He has but to come unto me and then ask, and he shall receive.

First he must come! The delay is with you, my sons and daughters.

This lesson is closed in love.

The Spiritual Quest

The Spiritual Quest

Series Five

V

The Spiritual Quest

LESSON 29

SPIRITUAL QUESTIONS

This is the lesson where I allow you to ask in spirit of me, and I will answer. This is for all men. If the shadow asks of me, there is no answer given for the spirit does not deal in the shadow realm. The spirit asks matters that concern the spirit, and thus, the answer is given freely. There are two questions upon your spirit at this time, and I will deal with both of them.

"Was the virgin birth truly what some men called it, namely, was the man Jesus of Nazareth born of a virgin woman, and if so, how was it done?" Is this not your first question?

Yes, it is!

Fine, here is the answer to your question.

Yes, the boy child born unto Mary was born of a virgin, and he grew to be the Christ of my great love, and I call him Son.

Now as to the matter of how! When man of the shadow deals with this matter, he seeks to find answers that fit his limited physical realm. For the physical shadow or form man, there can be no explanation that will satisfy him, so do not even attempt it. Matters of the spirit operate in a realm far above the earthly, and the two cannot be mixed in any fashion.

If Mary, the girl, had kept her form in control, then none of my spiritual givings could have taken place. She was a spirit-filled child and grew in her walk with me. She then had the freedom of communication with my Spirit even as you now experience with this writing. She knew of the need to bring into this world one who could in fullness express myself to all men. She then expressed the true desire to be the instrument of bringing forth the Christ Child. She received the seed of my Spirit, as was the one she was to bring forth. Her son and my Son, the Christ, then carried that knowing to the fullness of me, and the fully man was also fully the God Creator's Son. Mary held firmly the truth in her spiritual knowing, and as I have said in my spiritual law, when it is used properly by one of the spirit, it must produce what is held in the knowing. Christ was to be fully man, and therefore, she took all the time necessary to build the full child body within her body.

When the day came, she gave forth a son and named him Jesus, and he was of her love and not that of her husband, Joseph. He knew her not, nor was he to claim to be the father of the child. So it was that her son, who was fully man, and my Son, who was fully spirit, was born. He came that all men would follow his example and give themselves over to the control of my Spirit within them. And so committed as my sons and daughters, they too could share all that I have for them.

Jesus of Nazareth, the Christ, did not intend for man to lift him up to become the idol; he came to be the ideal. He did not mean for men to follow him and, thus, remain men of the flesh and form with no power of their own. He came so men and women would follow him as the example, and then with him as the example, they were to become once again the true spirit men and women of my creation. He said clearly these words that **all men and women are my children and are thus called sons and daughters of the Most High God**. "They will do even greater deeds than I have done," are also the words of my Son, the Christ. Do you now see with spiritual understanding? Do you now know with the spiritual sense of knowing that can only be a part of the spiritual child of my love, and thus knowing, will you claim the spiritual inheritance that awaits you?

The other question that you ask at this time is about the sense of the universal, for it is the last of the five key spiritual senses that I spoke of in an earlier word [Lesson 25] from my Spirit. I will tell you now what it is you are asking, but know that this answer is still limited because of the growth that is still before you.

The sense of the universal is the sense that is employed by one who has become one with my Spirit. Christ had the sense of the universal, and so he dealt with men in a way so as to prepare them for all the matters of the universal sense. Knowing, being, truth, and love, these when used to their fullness prepare you for matters of the universal for with this sense, you are broadened beyond the scope of this earthly man and his spiritual future. The spirit man will have a sense of my total creation and the worlds upon worlds that are beyond his range of comprehension. Let me say there are worlds for you to discover that would seem to be like paradise to the shadow man, but the spiritual man's sense of the universal allows him to take in a wide range of my activity of love. To say to men of the shadow, "There are other worlds and other galaxies of life and other universes beyond the range of the one you know, have, or think exists," is to create spiritual truth gaps for that child of my love, and thus, you would make it even harder for him on the road of his spiritual quest.

I have but opened the door of this question, and a ray of light has come forth. Let him, who will, come unto the light, and when he enters through the door of the universal, it will no longer be a world of my children that stand before him in need that he sees, but worlds untold with multi-levels of spiritual growth and need. You will find when the sense of the universal is a part of your spiritual sensing, each new world in the spirit that is made victorious is but the foundation for the next world of my great love.

I have said all I can at this time on the matter of your question. Seek in the spirit, and you will find, for I am spirit, and I await your arrival.

The lesson ends in a question as it began.

When will you come unto me?

LESSON 30

SPIRITUAL JOY

Write, for when the pleasure of God is seen in all things, then the spiritual joy of my being has become a part of the one who knows such pleasure in me.

I have told you of my joy and its overflowing and what must be done for you to experience such overflowing. I now wish to give you a clear understanding of joy in my Spirit. You must know from the beginning that the form man cannot hold as a part of his being my spiritual joy. So because the spirit at his center quickens him to know that it is obtainable, yet now beyond him, man will either give himself over to the spirit and, thus, obtain my spiritual joy, or he will substitute things of his own and call them by the name of joy. The things man calls joy are as unreal as the form man himself is. Let me clearly say there are no things of the earth that can give man spiritual joy. Therefore, spiritual joy cannot be his by anything he may gather from over the face of the earth. There are no deeds of the earth that can give man spiritual joy. Therefore, man cannot "do" any earthly feat and be filled with my joy. There are no conditions of being for the physical man to know my joy.

Therefore, there are no exercises of the body or mind that will allow the earthly man or woman to know my spiritual joy. Can you now see that the deeds and the thoughts of the form man will at their best leave man empty with the gnawing of the spirit going on within him? Reject these words if you will, but they are the truth, and they will not be altered for any fleshly man. There is no reality in him at all. Things of the spirit are for the spirit man, and they are reality and can be nothing other than what I have said.

When the joy of my Spirit is in a man or woman, there are signs that make it clear to that one that they are once again walking with me.

My joy lifts my child above the cares of the world. Joy is not a spiritual condition that makes the cares of the world vanish, but joy is the first step for my spiritual child to remove them. When you are living down with the worldly cares, you cannot remove them; you become a part of them. Joy lifts my child above the cares of this world so he may clearly deal with them and, one by one, remove them. Spiritual joy allows you to say in truth, "I am in this world, but not of it." Joy, then, is the ability to stand firmly upon the ground I call my Rock, while all the ground around you is seen slipping away like the washing of the sand by the sea.

Joy gives the mind a new clarity for the tasks that are to be done by the mind's surge under the direction of the spirit. Joy gives the body a new surge of energy that is known surely and clearly by the one receiving this energy of my spiritual joy.

Joy is a necessary part of the chord that is sounded with love and that gives a peace within the being that has been so filled. Love alone will not bring peace within. Joy alone will not bring peace within. Spirit love

Spiritual Joy

and spirit joy together will bring a spirit peace that is a thrill to this child of my creation. Now a great new truth that is in fact not new to me at all: When the peace comes to man caused by spiritual joy and love, that peace sets off a vibration that gives energy to both the love and the joy. They then are accelerated and heightened and go forth from man with greater force and power, only to return unto that same child with increased force and power of love and joy. This makes a deeper peace within, and thus, the cycle is repeated again, each time stronger than the one before. The spiritual vortex is set up that will finally make of this child of mine a spiritual being full of love, joy, and peace. When you are thus filled, you are more and more a capacity for the filling.

Do you not see there is growth in the spirit child and we are becoming more and more one? When we are in the spirit, then all that I have for you is yours to use and be. My Son the Christ learned this spiritual law and became the fullness of me, and thus, he was able to do all that he did before men. There was much more that he was able to do, but those around him were limited in their knowing and understanding. Therefore, he was not able to do all that he wanted to accomplish.

When the spirit men of my true new age become full and do greater deeds than were done by my Son the Christ (for he has said, "Greater deeds than I have done will you do"), know that he had far more spiritual ability than he was able to employ with the people of his day. If they were awed almost to the point of fear by simple deeds, what would have become of them if far greater deeds were done by him? Know this: My spiritual joy is a key to your becoming what I have planned for you.

"My joy is a gift of my love and is yours when you return unto me. You cannot earn it by any earthly act or deed. You have but to come unto me and receive the joy of your salvation," saith the Lord thy God.

This lesson ends, so let your joy begin now in me.

LESSON 31

SPIRITUAL PROSPERITY

Write, for this day will be full of productivity, and we will cover as many lessons as you are able to receive of me.

There has been great confusion for many years over the matter of spiritual prosperity. The earthly man, trying to become spiritual by his many ways of searching, sees the man of the flesh who has given control to the form with great wealth as he lives in luxury. He asks, "Why is it he has so much and lives totally for himself while I'm trying to live for you, Father, and I have little of this world's goods? It seems that God the Father is blessing with substance those who have rejected him and gives little substance to those trying to serve him."

"These are not the words of the living God, but the words of men," saith the Lord God.

Then man for a season decided that in order to be spiritual, he must give up all care for material wealth. He then said, "I will have nothing of the worldly goods in order to be more like God." These words could not be further from the truth. If I am the maker of all and therefore, all is of me, how then could man be more like me by having less and less?

A rich man came unto my Son Jesus of Nazareth and was told to take all that he had and give it unto the poor, and then he was to follow after the Christ and would find the true kingdom. Men still today use that truth of Christ to excuse themselves from the responsibility I have for them.

Jesus of Nazareth was not saying that the man was to become poor in order to follow him; he was saying, in fact, the man was to give himself over fully to the spirit, and then the things of the earth would have no value for him. Then the young man could follow the path before him in Christ. If earthly riches are, to the spirit child, things of no value because of the real he has found by being of the spirit, then for that child it is as if he has nothing of the earthly goods in terms of his placement of value upon them.

That is the condition that must be reached by my child if he is to be filled of me. If there is any place in him giving value to things, then I cannot be full in that one because of the things he still gives value to. If my child places no value on anything of the earth and places all value on the matters of the spirit, then we can be one in the spirit, and I will be able to fill his life with the presence of my Spirit.

Now let me speak of prosperity in true terms of the child filled of me. "The spirit-filled child is then ready to have great physical wealth for it will be no more than a tool in his hands to help raise his brothers and sisters in my Spirit," saith the Lord thy God. I am pleased to give great wealth to my spirit children for their use of the substance will be pleasing unto me and their brothers and sisters will hear and learn of me by the spending of that wealth. Man of the spirit moves in a physical

Spiritual Prosperity

plane called earth living, and it is my intention to give him every means to help him in his efforts to call others unto me.

There are means of communication that can reach millions at one time for me. When you are prepared to share my truth with men of the world, you will have every earthly tool to help you in your spiritual task. Would the Lord God send you out with empty hands and, thus, insure your task to be long and difficult, or would I give you great abundance so all men could see the full spirit man as he labors for me?

Do not try and measure the substance in amounts for it will always be sufficient for the task you do in the spirit. If your labor requires pennies to accomplish the task, then pennies will be your tools. If millions are required for your task, then prepare yourself for the task, for when you are ready, you may know the millions have been waiting for you and not you waiting for them. You have but to ask of me knowing, and it shall be yours. Only the spirit may know; therefore, only the spirit-filled child will have his requests filled to overflowing.

The spirit does not ask for millions when pennies will supply the need. Know this every one of you, that as you have given control over to the spirit and the form is being directed by the Spirit which is of me, the form will have use of all that the Spirit doth allow. "Look upon the life of King Solomon, and know that it was not wealth that he sought, but my Spirit," saith the Lord. He became wise in the spirit, and as he so walked with me, he was able to share my truth with his people. I then gave him wealth that he could not count, and his storehouse was filled to an overflow. His people did not go hungry even while famine was known to surround them. They knew a spiritual peace as long as they did not seek to rule by way of the form.

When, however, the spirit was no longer allowed to direct their paths, soon the wealth was gone, and they became a people scattered and starving, and all of the great wealth had turned to dust.

You must know this for it is a warning to all who have ears of the Spirit. Walk with me, and you walk in abundance, for I am abundant and I am the Lord thy God. Walk alone on your own path, and even what little you do have will vanish from you. I will not take it from you for I am the Lord and I am the Giver. When you walk as the shadow, then your own kind will take that which you have. Darkness does not give; it only takes. Light cannot take; it only gives.

I am light, and you are light when you walk and live in me.

Let my spiritual child ask anything of me, and know that the supply of his asking is on the way as he began his request. You need not repeat the request. Hold firm to the knowing that it is yours and not to the request itself. For when you hold to the request, you have to let go of the knowing, and thus, the request cannot be filled, and thus, you need to ask again. If you hold to the knowing, then the request cannot be anything but filled. Let the spirit request of the Spirit and so receive. Let the form of the shadow request of the Spirit, and know it has gone no higher than the top of his head and cannot be filled.

The lesson ends. Your riches await you!

LESSON 32

THE DISPLEASURE OF GOD

Write.

I am a loving God to the fullness of love. I am a patient God with no limitation to my patience. There are matters that displease me, and I share them with you in order that my love for you may more effectively draw you unto myself. I made a paradise world for the spiritual man of my creative handiwork, and I placed him within it with all power to build upon that paradise. He was to use my spiritual powers for the good of all that came to this spiritual being. It was displeasure to me when man turned from me and placed his control in the hands of the form. In so doing, man gave up nearly all of the power my love had given unto him. An unlimited spiritual being had become a very limited form.

You ask, "Are the sins of man, the flesh or form, a displeasure to me?" and I answer, "I do not even look upon them. They are sins of the shadow of the real, and there is no spiritual reality in any of the earthly man's doings." What he calls good and what he calls bad, I say, to the spirit do not exist at all. Even the matters that the form man calls displeasures unto God are as false as is the form man himself. Even when I am displeased, I give my abundant love to the one who displeases me. Even an earthly father says he loves the child of his who sins, but he is displeased by that which he calls sin.

I am also displeased when the form of one tries to take and lead one of my spiritual children from me. He has compounded his rebellion by causing the spirit rebellion of another to become real. Thus, another child of my Spirit has yielded control to the form. There will be much hurt and agony upon them, but let it be said that even in my displeasure, I do not give forth anything but my love. The hurt and agony that come upon the shadow of the real man are put upon him by his own hand.

There is yet another matter that brings displeasure before me. That is the matter you know as the sin against the Holy Spirit.

I have already made it clear to you that all the sins of the flesh are sins of the shadow of the real, and they are gone the moment the spirit returns unto me. For then, those who gave the shadow of the real its power of control have taken that same control and placed it in the hands of the spirit of my Spirit, and therefore, those sins are to me as if they had never been. I do not look upon them now or ever more!

It displeases me when the spirit man, whom I made in full love, rejects my Spirit and will not allow the spiritual oneness to take place. For this spirit one has come to a place where he knows of the spirit and, in his own rebellious pride of spirit, wishes to be alone. He does not give control to the fleshly form, though that alone could give him much grief. He in spirit rejects the very source that gave him reality to begin with. I will strive in spirit to call this one unto me, but when that spirit says,

The Displeasure of God

"No," in final rejection, there occurs a full and final loss of that spirit.

It is like a branch that says to the vine that gives it life, "I now separate myself from you," and thus, the spirit dies, for I am spirit, and there is no source other than myself for I am the Lord thy God and I am all. That spirit will never know life at all, and the form returns unto the dust for without the spirit, it cannot be perfected. That spirit goes from eternal existence and life to eternal nonexistence you would call death. That is the only true death there is, and when it occurs, it is a displeasure to my Spirit for I am spirit. It is pain, sorrow, and even agony for the shadow of the real to be in control while the spirit remains in its rebellious state, but woe be unto the spirit that rejects the Spirit of the Lord God. That spirit will finally be nonexistent if he or she persists to the end of the rebellion.

The man of the form has called the sin against the Holy Spirit many things, and he can give an equal number of examples. Know ye now that when the shadow casts around him the very best that he has, there is yet nothing to be found but more shadow.

That which is not real cannot give forth anything that is real. May that which is a displeasure unto another cause a stirring of your spirit, and may it call you to come unto me so you may know the joy that was mine in your making, and may you receive all that is for your spirit of my Spirit. Thus saith the Lord thy God, for I am the Creator, and my Word calleth all men unto me. I am the Author and the Finisher of all that is good.

"As this lesson is closed, may you open to the call of my Spirit," saith the Lord God of love.

The Spiritual Quest

LESSON 33

THE MATTER OF TRUTH

Write.

"Truth is spiritual, eternal, all there is that comes forth from me," saith the Lord God of all men. Truth brings light unto dark places. Truth is higher than any climb of man's mind, yet he has but to come unto me, and my knowing is his to call upon. My knowing is all truth.

Truth of the Spirit is how things are and not what they seem to be to men of the earth. Truth is that part of me that sets men free, for anything less than truth binds man to it.

Do you see that truth will set men free, for neither their coming nor their going will change any part of it?

Man of the spirit soon learns that truth is all that is ever given in the spirit, and the earthly man can never arrive at full truth by any means other than the Spirit's giving. Any word that seeks to bind man to it cannot then, by its nature, be what it claims.

Truth places a man freely in the center of a field and says, "All that the eye can behold is yours." Walk and listen to me, and you will always be free for it is my nature to set man free indeed. The man who holds truth in his grasp is the spirit man.

The shadow of truth, which I call lie or half-truth, locks man in a cell and says, "You must stay here in order for you to receive the truth that I have for you." So man is bound by a lie called "truth," and the more he accepts, the smaller his prison cell. One day, he awakens to find the four walls of his false truth have closed in upon him, and he now is unable to move at all. He cries out, "You have lied to me. I am not free. I am more bound than on the day we began this terrible walk together." Many a man has walked the path of half-truths of other men, only to find they are destructive at the end of his journey. "Woe is me; I am undone!" is his cry, and finally, his cry is a truth. But who is nearby to hear his crying? Walk the street where the gutter and the hallway are lined with my children who have listened to the false call of other men, and you will see the result of a walk outside of my truth. To these, my children, you can offer the truth of my Spirit, but they are so tuned to accepting a lie and calling it truth that they will but reject the truth of my Spirit and call it a lie.

How then are you to reach them with my truth?

"Is there a way?" you say.

There is, because even at the very center of every one of these children there is my Spirit. It will require the Spirit and truth of me with much power to break through the cell and chains that bind this child of my love. Know this as you look upon the degenerate child before you: My love for that one is as great as my love you know within yourself. It is the nature of false truths to use every means to attract man away from me. The greater the employment of earthly things used to prove the truth before you, the greater the lack of truth. These words are naught but lies and half-truths. A lie is that which has no spiritual truth to it at all. To say, "God loves only those who follow his Son the Christ and does not love any of the others," would be speaking a lie. To say, "God loves all men, but loves some more than others," is the use of a half-truth. When man says, "God loves all men," that is truth, but to say, "God loves some more than others," is a lie, and I do not speak in lies or in half-truths.

In an earlier lesson, I spoke of some of the basics of my truth, and for that series of lessons, it was all that was needed to be said. Now that our lessons have taken us further in our spiritual quest, I speak of deeper aspects of that same truth. Truth is like a deep pool of water: the deeper one goes, the greater the force available to that one who is deepened in me. I am truth, and so as one goes more deeply in my truth, the deeper he finds himself in new areas of knowing. When a man begins to operate at a deeper level of truth, the more of my revelation will be opened unto him.

Would you agree that man has come far in the last five hundred years? "Yes," say most men, "we have come far in the past five hundred years."

I say unto you, "Man has changed very little in these past five hundred years. If he goes into my truth to new depths, he will make strides that are of true value to all men." I speak from a spiritual base, not from the physical.

Spiritual man can heal all sickness without blade or medication, and this is a truth of deeper nature. Spiritual man will control all the elements around him, and they will yield to his very wish; this is a truth of a deeper nature. Spiritual man will create new industries for the good of all mankind, and he will build and develop the earth, not destroy it as the earthly man is doing even at this very hour. This, too, is a deeper truth.

There are worlds for the spirit man to build and develop, and he will know of higher life forms and work with them to make a better place for his own kind. Spirit man will see with new eyes things of my handiwork that are yet beyond the dreams of the man of this day. This is a truth.

If the shadow man, or the form, keeps the control that he now has, he will soon have used up his present known resources, and he will have destroyed the very system that has sustained him. These words are a truth of my Spirit.

I would now speak of one final matter which shall be a filling to your spirit. I said that truth is like a deep pool of water, and the deeper one goes, the greater the pressures that are found there. Truth is a force that is able to create a pressure ratio between light and its vibration, which is of me, and my love vibration, which together caused the earth to be formed for man to live upon. It was the vibration of my love that sent out the vibration of my light, which was directed by the pressure vibration of my truth, and the impact of light upon light created the carbon base out of which your planet earth came forth. This is a truth of deeper giving, and one day, your men of science will discover what is already upon this page.

These words are a truth for all men. Come unto me for I have much more to share with you, my children. I speak in truth, and the lesson ends.

LESSON 34

WORLD PEACE

Write.

"There will be wars and rumors of wars." Is not this the truth of my Word to man ages ago?

He has not yet learned the lesson that would end wars forever upon the face of this planet. Hear my words clearly, for <u>I will now tell you of a plan that shall bring an end to all wars!</u> It will not come to pass as long as the spirit-filled men are kept to the sidelines of world activity. As long as the form man is in control, there will be wars upon wars, and each will be more destructive than the one before.

Peace cannot be maintained by the making of new weapons of destruction. Peace is not the absence of war, but the chord of harmony of love of the spirit and joy of that same spirit. The spirit man has placed his values on the spiritual; therefore, neither the land nor the holdings of another could cause him to war with his brother.

The spirit man lives above the world structures created by the mind of man, and therefore, all the isms by the most brilliant minds hold no cause for him. Why would a man of spiritual knowing give himself to any cause that has no true knowing in it at all?

The spirit man will not war over issues of value given by other men when he holds all that is of true value already. Would a man with a diamond in hand, knowing of its true value, exchange it for a lump of earth that can be washed away at the first rain? No, he would hold onto what he already has for the offer of the earthen lump is of no value to him.

The spirit man is the true man of peace, for he has it within himself, and it has become a part of his being, just like his physical life is dependent upon his breathing. I have given you enough to see the spirit man will not war with his brother; in fact, he cannot for the spirit and the war are as far apart as are the shadow man and the spirit, or the real, man. Men then ask, "How then is the world to come to a place of full and final peace?" Quickly these same men will rise up and say, "Let us sit at a table with other men of the world, and we will work out a peace." That is the external working towards the internal, and it has not brought peace unto men through the centuries. It has, at its best, brought pauses between wars called peace by men.

I say unto you now that we shall let the internal work toward the external, and men of my Spirit will go into every country of the world, and by their deeds of power and words of truth, they will change men one by one. Some will be called to bring spiritual change to the laborer of the field, and he will use a new spiritual power as he works the soil. Others will establish new businesses that give rather than take, and they will build new opportunities for every man. The goods they develop will make it a better place, and the spirit men will grow in number.

Their voice will be heard first softly, but later like the thunder of the spring storm. When they speak, the earth will be silent, and the voice of God will be heard. Then these servants of the spirit will add to their number.

Some will call upon the men in high places, and they will turn from their shadow ways unto the ways of the spirit. All that they have gained to this point will be like rags to be set aside so the suit of the spirit might be worn. Men will begin to wear the robe of royal blue. This will grow from the high place to the low and all places in between. This will grow from the inner to the outer. A man will be changed. Men will be changed. A nation will be changed. Nations will be changed, a world will be changed, and then this earth will know peace.

Is it over, then, when this great hour of victory has come?

"No," I say unto you, "it is not the ending; it is but the beginning." Spirit men will then make new discoveries that will give mankind great advancement. It will become a paradise on earth, and there man must be careful for he will have but restored the earth to its place of true beginning. Then my full plan for man of the earth will be able to begin.

Do you think all of this will be without resistance? Do you think the forces of evil will not try all the harder to take men aside from their new path of the spirit? They will once again, as before, try to turn men from me so they may become again men of the shadow while the spirit awaits again for the return of peace to this earth. I tell you now if man turns again from his form and gives the spirit the true place in his life and then again returns the power to the form, he will know war that will make this planet a place unfit at all for man. Ages will pass, and the remnant will build a new world of peace, and they will observe this planet and will say, "Here is the earth where man once lived, but now it is barren, and all has become dust of his handiwork. Earth is now like Mars and those planets before it."

I speak to you in the sense of the universal, which is beyond the man of the shadow.

Let there be peace upon this earth of my creation. Let there be peace among men. Let the peace begin in you.

The lesson ends in the peace of my Spirit, which is for all men.

LESSON 35

GOD'S POWER

May we begin? Write.

Let it be known by every man that the power of God is available to every spiritual child who walks the path of the Lord. The form who rules his spirit will have none of my power available to him. Man asks what God's power is, and I answer in spirit it is all there is. Power is that energy and vibration of my Spirit that cause my spiritual desire to go forth unto completion. The power of God is the still point of the universal from which all has its beginning. Earthly man has always associated power with *might, strength,* and *vigorous activity,* but I say it is none of these things, nor are they even near the true understanding of the power of God. All of man's descriptions are based upon the areas of his physical senses, and since his senses are so limited, his description cannot go beyond those same limitations. I ask you now some simple questions of the spirit, and let it be your spirit that answers me.

Which has more power, the earthly man, who with all his *might* comes thundering down upon the spiritual man to do him harm, or the spiritual man, who stands calmly in his spiritual knowing? In the spiritual man's knowing is the truth that the might of the enemy cannot touch even one hair upon his head. The enemy will soon exhaust his might, and the spirit man will not even have lifted one finger to his own defense. When Daniel faced the den of lions or when the three men Shadrach, Meshach, and Abednego stood in the fires of the furnace, was not the might of men hurled upon them? Did they as spiritual men resist at all, or did they know they were in the protective hand of God?

I answer, "Power is in knowing."

I say then not the might of men, but the knowing of the Spirit of God contains the true power that I speak of, and your spirit speaks the truth. Man then moves on to the next earthly power, and he employs his *strength* to build, and day after day, year after year, he builds his cities and temples at great cost and with the use of great strength. The spirit man, with his sense of being, is eternal, and in time when all the cities have been cleared to build new ones and the temples are nowhere to be found, the spirit man stands eternal without change, and he knows his being to be the true temple of the living God. The spirit man has not had to give of his strength to stand eternal; his sense of being, which can only be had by the spiritual man, is alone sufficient throughout all eternity. In which of these two do you find the power?

The power is in the sense of being, which is of God.

You answer again in true spirit.

Yet a third time I ask you in the following manner: A body of men went into the temple to pray. There was great activity in their praying. They prayed loudly so all could hear and so they could be an example for others around them to follow. They then went forth and gathered funds to give to the needy, and all saw the work of their gathering. They then returned to the temple and, night after night, told others of their prayers and deeds of good works, and all that heard and saw did agree that there was a great work being accomplished, and they were men giving *great activity* in the name of the Lord.

There was yet another man of common origin who prayed in quiet, and even those nearby were unable to detect his spiritual request. He did not go out of his way to find anyone, but only dealt with the persons or matters that came before him. If food was the need, he gave forth food that came from him as freely as he gave forth his power. He met the need of men with love, and though there was little activity to be seen by anyone, he was power. Not by what he gave off, but by the quiet stillness from within was the power known to be present. True power after use has more remaining than when it was first used.

The power of God is to gain in giving, and it is without activity and not the excess of it.

Again you have allowed the spirit to speak for you, for now you know, and thus, there is spiritual power over man's might. You are a spiritual being, and thus, you have power over the strength of the earthly form man. In love, there comes forth from the still point a giving that increases both the giver and the receiver. The power of man then decreases with its use while the power of God increases with its use, and its use comes out of the still point of quiet, not out of the place of much activity.

If men would know the power of God, then let them ground their arms and know I am the Lord God of all and there is no power outside of myself. If men would know power, let them come unto me, and their knowing will be the might of their using. If men would know the power of God, let my sense of being come upon them, and then the strength of all men cannot compare with their sense of being. If men would know the power of the Lord God, let them go to the center of themselves where there is stillness and not activity, and there they will find love of the spirit, and they will be a part of the power they seek. Have I not said, "It is all there is"? Then is there more than what I have declared unto you? Know that with the use of my power, there is no loss, only gain on the part of all involved, both as giver and receiver.

"The lesson and the series end upon these words: Guide the men who will come unto me, for the power that I am is theirs for the asking, but first they must come unto me," thus saith the Lord God of love, power, and stillness.

The Spiritual Quest

Series Six

VI

The Spiritual Quest

LESSON 36

DEEPER MEANINGS OF LIFE

Whenever we speak of the word *life*, man of the shadow quickly responds that he knows what it is and how it should be handled.

To the earthly man, life is that period of physical activity of man before his death. Life then is short or long depending upon the time of one's death. Life to these same individuals is measured by how one lives until death comes. All of life is then based upon one single event called death.

If a person has a great deal of physical wealth, he lives life richly, and if he has very little or no goods at all, it is said that he lives life very poorly. There are all stages between these two extremes. Life is also then based on the abundance or scarcity of substance. Things help to determine one's life.

Third, man of the shadow speaks of life being happy or sad, full of fun or the lack of it, and many other expressions that are the measurements of life's standards. He then sets standards by the measurement of his mind. Then he conducts his life by these standards. He works, saves, and plans for the day when he can rest from his labor and relax and enjoy life. This is, in his mind, a very brief period before the arrival of death.

If man of the shadow is "religious," he speaks of a life after death, and if not, he believes that it all ends with his death. Again there are variations to these two extremes. Men of the shadow can look at these words and find themselves somewhere in between each of the conditions described.

I would speak to you now in spiritual terms as to the reality of life: what it truly is, how it is to be lived, its relationship to earthly values, and its comparison to the false structure of the shadow man you call earthly.

Life is the real presence of the Spirit within every man. I have placed that part of my Spirit which is eternal in every man, and it is that part of me that gives and sustains the life within the form. The activity of the form is not life. There could be no form activity, however, without life. Life is then the love of God given to every man. For anything to be real, it must be eternal. If the subject is temporal in any way (meaning it is here now, but in several hundred, thousand, or million years it will be gone), then it cannot be called real. Reality never ends. Life of the spirit is real; it will never end. You may discard the form, or body, in a thousand different ways, but the spirit within the form is real, and therefore, it will never end. Anything that is real must have eternity as a part of its true form.

What then is life?

Life is that spirit part of the creator that is in every human person. I am the Lord thy God, and I am forever. Life then is that spirit of God in man that makes him different from all other creatures. All other creatures have an existence, but it is not the same as life in the spirit. Man, when he rejects God, moves from an earthly life to an earthly existence that lives without life. There is a great deal of difference between the two terms. Earthly existence is temporal; life in the spirit is eternal. Man the shadow can breathe and move and be said to be living without life. Man the spirit is living by his breathing and moving, but he is a holder of life that is eternal and a part of his own being. If man is perfected, then his living and his life of the spirit have become one, and that perfected one has his living continue on in his life, which is of the spirit. If man is not perfected, then his living can end, but his life goes on eternally. And thus, it can be said that a man may end his living, but he can never end his life, for it is eternal.

If life then is real, which it is, we may ask, "How then is it to be lived?" The real must live in relationship with all else that is real. Therefore, your life goes on as it relates to and is guided by all that is real by the hand and will of God the Creator. The moment your life is related to the unreal, which is the life of things around you, I say unto you your life in the Spirit of God has ended and your living or existence has begun. You may call it "life," but it is not life to me, and so I call it by what it really is, existence.

"Life and earthly values are not in the same realm at all, and so you may exist and be living with much earthly goods and not have had an experience of life as I know it," saith the Lord thy God.

Earthly things are not in the spiritual realm; they are beneath it. For the spirit man, the things of the earth are but tools to be used and are given no value by his spirit. I did not say man was to withdraw from the earth in order to be spiritual. I said you can be in the earth, but not of it. Things of the earth are temporal as even the earth itself is temporal.

Things of the spirit are eternal and, therefore, not of the earth at all.

Man says life is physical activity, and I say unto you living may be physical activity, but life is of my Spirit and is the still point within every man. Man says life is lived richly or poorly by the abundance of things or the lack of them. I say unto you life is spiritual and eternal and is not measured by things at all for things are limited and life is eternal.

If the mind-and-body man, called the shadow, becomes the spirit man of my original making, then the living form may become one with the spirit life, and when the oneness is complete, both in oneness will be eternal. Prepare thyself to begin your true living in the spirit I call life, and that life is eternal.

LESSON 37

LOVE'S DEEPER MEANING

Write.

Love is a spiritual causer, and I speak of the deep and abiding love that I have for you as my children. I love equally those of you who rebel and turn from me as I do those of you who turn unto me and begin your spiritual climb back to our original oneness.

Love is a vibration of such frequency that there is no equipment of man that can record its reality. You can, however, observe various results of my love when it is properly applied.

Let me clear up some misunderstandings of the mind level of love, for this is as high as the physical, or the shadow, of the real man can go.

When man speaks of love for food or things, it is not love of the spirit, but a physical-to-physical kind of vibration. It is one that can be observed, and man has done many strange things when moved by this vibration of the very lowest kind. If one deals with other persons at this level of relationship, you have, in fact, made a person into an object or a thing, and this is not creative or constructive at all.

There is also a vibration of love that gives and receives with each dependent upon the other, for example, "I love you if you love me, and we love each other by receiving and giving in a form of exchange." If, however, one stops giving, then the other stops receiving, and as he or she stops receiving, he or she then stops giving, and thus, the dependency is ended, and the love vibrations end with it. It is not a consuming love, but it is a very interdependent love. This interdependent love is not the love of the spirit that was used by my Spirit in my act of creation.

The spirit love is all giving to the very fullest measure. It does not end, nor is it taken away, when the child that is to receive it rejects it from the sender. Man of the shadow has known about this love as it was used by the Greeks and was given the word *agape*. I speak now not about a high level of mind knowing, but of a true level of spirit experiencing.

Man of the flesh can only know about my love for him in this way, for he has turned from me and prevents my love from moving within him. Only men and women of the Spirit can experience this love that I speak of, and once experienced, just its mention brings a thrill to the hearts of my spiritual children.

Know this: The experience of my love allows you as my children to give it forth to all as well. Can you see that a love that is intended for all cannot come upon you, be received by you, and not be passed on to others? That which was sent out to all must be passed on to all.

Yes, even those who reject you, your words, or even your love will not be able to hold out against us forever. Did you not know that it was my love for you and others who loved you with my same love for you that brought you back unto me? "Yes," I say unto you all, "it is my love that is constant and full and that turns man finally away from his way of folly back unto the Creator of all that is good."

I now speak of this same love in higher terms still. It is not a different love that I speak of, but the same love with greater intensity. My love, when used properly, is a protective shield that has such an intense vibration to it that nothing created by the man of the form can penetrate through it. Yes, man could even be fired upon and nothing would strike him, and if it did, there would be no sign of damage to his physical form.

Let us increase the intensity still more, and one day, men of science will find that it is this vibration of my love that holds all the atoms in place as well as the stars and planets in their paths of flight. It is an ordered universe in which your planet is found to be, and it is my love that holds the order of which I speak.

Let us go to still another range of intensity of my love. As I said in another lesson, my love is that which will bring the real down to manifest form, and when man reaches that intensity of love and he is spirit of my Spirit, he too will be a creator as I have said he is.

At yet another intensity of my love vibration, man will be able to move from one place to another like light now moves from one star to another. It will appear to the physical man, who has turned from me, that the spirit man of my love has disappeared and then later reappeared. He will not have gone out of sight at all, but only out of the range of sight of the shadow man. The real men and women with this vibration can move from place to place with ease.

Now I tell you a truth that you may find difficult, but yet it is true. If the vibration of my love reaches another intensity, the man or woman of my love will move to new dimensions now totally unknown to the men and women of your planet.

There are many more usages for my love, and as you grow, you will know more and more. All that I have spoken in these pages is available to the one who will read these words of mine. Do not ask, "How can it be so?" Do not say, "It is not so." You will not change the truth of my Spirit by your rejection of it; you only delay your own spiritual awakening.

These series of lessons are being prepared to call the shadow of the real (man of the flesh) back unto the love of the Creator and to make of you new men and women, men and women of the spirit.

I have so much more for you, but until you have made use of what I have given you thus far, there is no value for me to tell you more. It will only bring you to a greater frustration. This is not my intention through this lesson. I love you, my child, and I will always love you. I call you to come unto me and to allow me to give you all that I have prepared for you. It has been waiting, lo, these many centuries as have I.

As the lesson on my love's deeper meanings comes to a close, I say to you, "Come, for my arms are open wide to receive you."

LESSON 38

SPIRITUAL UNTO PHYSICAL MANIFESTATION

Know ye this: I am prepared now to speak of a matter that can give unto the spiritual man a great power, for I will make man of the spirit a creator. It should be clear to you by now that the gifts of the Spirit are for the spirit man only. The man of the earth, called the shadow of the real, will never have this power available to him. He can even read the steps required for manifestation and memorize every spiritual word and still the ability will elude him. This is a spirit power available only to men and women of the spirit. It is for every man and woman because every man and woman on this earth are in reality my children, and they are spirit in me, for I am spirit. Only their turning from me keeps these laws of truth from their grasp. Could the runner stand at the starting line, with all the ability to win the dash, and win by running in the opposite direction of the race? "No," you would quickly say, "he must run the prescribed course from start to finish." So it is in the terms of the spirit. There is a prescribed course, and it must be run from the start to the finish if you are to be included in all that the race provides. I am spirit, and all of my gifts are spiritual, and therefore, man of the flesh cannot involve himself in these matters. Man of the spirit has but to ask of me, and his requests are fulfilled. They are fulfilled even while he is asking, for I know his need even while he expresses it before me.

Man of the flesh can stand by and say, "I see nothing and I heard your request, so God did not answer you." How could any real request of the spirit go from request to physical reality before going through the proper steps of the spiritual law? The spiritual is real, and the physical reality is only a manifestation of the real; it is not the real itself. How then could a request of the spirit become form without first having been real?

"Let me now give you the steps of the spiritual law that will bring unto the spiritual man the requests of his heart," saith the Lord God of all gifts that are real.

First: The request of a need must come from a spirit-controlled child, woman, or man of any age, but they must have given their spirits control over their bodies for only the real to the real can bring about manifestation.

Second: The request must be needed and as real as the one doing the requesting. This is why the law is not available to the man or woman of the shadow or form. This power can only be entrusted to the one who has given the spirit control.

Third: The request must be clear and exact in the spirit one who comes before me to be able to do fully what is required. If you cannot be specific in your asking, even though I am able to give in clarity, you will not be able to receive in clarity, and therefore, you will not be able to do fully what is required of you.

Fourth: You must ask in the knowing, knowing that while you are asking, it is being given. The request will be manifested in direct relation to the fullness of your knowing. I speak not of partial knowing for you cannot hold this spiritual sense in part. I speak to the size of your spirit in its capacity at the time of your request. When my Son the Christ asked of me, he was the full spirit, and he was filled full of my Spirit; thus, we were one, and his manifestation was instant in its arrival. There are other examples in my Word where other spirit men, though full, contained less knowing, and thus, the manifestation took longer. There is a relationship between the knowing and the power to manifest that have each depending upon the other.

Fifth: You must hold with your knowing and with your spiritual sense of being the request that you have made of me. This is why I said in step three you must be clear and exact in your request. For now, your senses of knowing and being are joined by my love and giving. It is the Lord God that gives every request, and it is the spirit child of my Spirit that works with me to hold the reality of the request until the manifestation has taken form, and then there is no need to hold the real and true gift any longer. It is not abandoned and left alone, but this step is then completed.

Sixth: The real in the spirit is now brought down into a manifest form of the real, and this is done by love. Know this: Everything you now see in physical form you call real was first made in spirit for it is the spirit and not the manifestation that is the real.

Then my love brought it down from the real to the form of the real. It was in this way your earth and all of the stars that you see at night when you look up into the heavens were formed. Know this as well: It is still my love for you that holds your world together, for if the vibration of my love were removed from you, the earth would return from the manifest form unto the real. The world, as you know it, would vanish, though it would be unchanged in the real where I hold it even now by my love.

Seventh: You now bless in love the gift of your request and then use it as it was intended. If funds are needed, request what is needed. Do not ask for more or less than the need. I will give your request for funds. If they are slow in their arrival, know the delay is with you. Your spiritual knowing container must be increased, and then I will fill it full (I speak of you in the spirit), and your manifestation will appear more quickly.

The creation of things is one of the most simple for the full spirit of my Spirit. It is unreachable for the physical form man, for again I say unto you the matters of the earth are as far apart from the matters of the spirit as the stars in the heavens are from your planet called earth.

Do you wish to make real the requests of your spirit? Know that they are real as you apply this spiritual law.

The lesson ends, and your creation is before you.

LESSON 39

THE TRUE MEANINGS OF ABUNDANCE

I speak to you now of the spiritual realities of abundance and how this abundance is employed by the spirit man.

The spirit man is lead of the spirit, and therefore, his efforts, though they be at times physical, have a spiritual purpose as their goal. The physical man can hold much wealth and have no abundance at all. For the physical man, abundance means a possession of more than he can use or spend. For the spiritual man, abundance means the availability of much more for the work of the kingdom, and the spirit man grows in capacity and responsibility to use the abundance he has for spirit work. He does this only to find that he has grown and there is yet much more available for his using.

The abundance of God is ever increasing; the abundance of earthly man is ever decreasing. The abundance of God is eternal; the abundance of earthly man is temporal. The abundance of God is for the spirit man's using; the abundance of earthly man is for the earthly man's using. Abundance of the spirit makes all men more abundant if they receive of the spirit. Abundance of the earthly man makes no one more abundant and is used up in earthly use. Abundance of the spirit grows with use by the spirit man and cannot ever be used up.

Let us look now at some of the practical aspects of the two kinds of abundance. Know this: True abundance is spiritual, and false abundance is physical.

As man grows in spirit, he has more of God's abundance available to him. I have said several times before that the waiting for the abundance is with man and not with God, and this is the truth of my Word. Spiritual abundance has no limitation – none whatsoever! – and since this is true, the limitation is with the growing spirit child.

If the child is of the spirit, then all of my abundance is his. If then it is all his and yet he does not have it, why does he not have it? He has not claimed it at all, or he has claimed it wrongly. Have I not said knowing cannot be held in part? The spirit man has all knowing, but only to the capacity of his growth.

If one man came to me as a container smaller than the one I intended him to use, would I not fill what he brought unto me? Man then would have "all-knowing," all he is able to contain, but not all that is available from God the Giver. When the spirit man arrives, as did my Son the Christ, then he would stand before me in full capacity as I have made him, and he would then receive the fullness that I speak of in all knowing.

Each time the spirit man comes, he will be filled to capacity, and each

The True Meanings of Abundance

time there is a greater capacity. God's abundance is spirit man's opportunity for growth. The abundance of man must be looked after and cared for, or else it will rust and turn to dust, be stolen, or become a loss in a hundred different ways. The abundance of God remains in the ever-present spirit form, ready to be used upon command. I will tell you a parable of the two men of abundance.

One man had great wealth, and he required a servant to do nothing but look after the things he took along with him on a trip. Another servant was required to count and look after his money that he took with him on his journey. The rich man became suspicious of the two servants, and so on his trip, he spent one half of each day going over the things the first servant was responsible for.

The other half of each day was spent going over the things with the servant who was responsible for his money. By the time his trip had ended, he was exhausted from the responsibility of overlooking the overlookers of his abundance.

A second man went on a trip, and he was a spirit man that had all the abundance of his Creator. He got up each morning and spent one half of his day doing as he was led of the Spirit. At times he would rest; other times he would help someone around him to use his abundance. In this way, he would spend the remaining half of his day doing again as he was led of the Spirit. If funds were needed, funds were provided. If help, love, joy, patience, or kindness was required, it was given. At the end of his trip, he returned to his home full of love and joy. He was at peace with himself and his fellow men, and he returned rested, and his abundance was greater at the end of his trip than at the beginning of it.

The Spiritual Quest

Which of these two men had the true use of abundance? Do you not know that the true abundance is available to you? Jesus of Nazareth took loaves and fishes in his hands, broke and blessed them, and passed the pieces among the thousands. When all had eaten, there were baskets left over. There was more than when they started, and five thousand ate their fill besides. What he did, you can do and even more than this, for he spoke to you the truth. Jesus of Nazareth, my Son the Christ, used the law of my abundance to its fullness because he was full himself. The law he used is a spiritual one and can be employed by any man or woman of the spirit.

The same law cannot be used by the shadow man, though he may try with all the strength within him. Let me now give you the spiritual law used by Christ, and I say unto you if you use the same spiritual law, it will work for you in abundance.

First: The law is a spirit law and can only be applied by a man or woman of the spirit.

Second: The law is as limited, or as abundant, as is the spirit user.

Third: The need must be presented before the user of the law. To use it as an exercise or to give proof to another is to abuse the law, and an abuser will no longer be a user.

Fourth: In spirit, the need must be brought before me.

Fifth: In spirit, the user of the law must bless and give thanks for the use of the spiritual law.

Sixth: The user must hold the need firmly before me by his spirit.

Seventh: The user shares from the abundance freely with all who are in need, and the supply will be full, and there will be an abundance greater than when he first began.

Jesus of Nazareth, the Christ and my Son, used the law of abundance, and all were fed. You may use the same law when you walk in the spirit and apply the steps that I have given you above.

This lesson ends with the truth that to the man of the spirit, his abundance awaits him.

The Spiritual Quest

LESSON 40

SENSING: PHYSICAL AND SPIRITUAL

I have given you a great deal on this matter in my earlier letters to you that I used to prepare you for these spiritual lessons. At the close of this lesson, I will tell you what you are to do when the series of seven are all complete. I give you the instructions because by the end of this lesson, your spiritual senses will have been employed, and thus, there is true value in giving over the instructions at this time.

According to you as men of the earth, the physical senses used by man of the shadow are five. They are called by me but four for I have given you the sense of refreshment and you have divided it into two senses called the sense of taste and the sense of smell. They are in reality only one sense.

There are a total of thirteen senses available to man. Yes, I say *thirteen*, and you use even poorly only four (or five if you go by your own figures). I will speak of all thirteen senses in this lesson, but I wish to give emphasis on five key senses that are ready to be used by the spirit man and are beyond the use of the physical man. The use of these five is very important for when they are employed, I can then take the spirit child much further and with greater clarity by their use. For example, if I spoke of something you accept without reservation, but spoke it to people two hundred years past, as you know years, they would resist the truth with great vigor. They would not change the position of the truth, but only delay it for themselves.

Let us look now at the thirteen senses of the spiritual man. But first the four (man says five) senses that are employed by the earthly man are hearing, touch, sight, and refreshment (smell and taste).

First: *Physical hearing* is a very narrow range of sensing. The sound waves are picked up by the outer ear, carried to the inner ear, and then translated by the brain, and the sound impulse thus picked up is translated into what you know as sound. This is called physical hearing.

Second: There is another sense of the spirit called *spiritual perceiving*; this gives man a much wider range and permits him to pick up beyond his present range of the ear.

Third: The sense of touch, which is on the surface, or what is called by man *physical touch*. It is the one he presently employs. There are two other senses of touch that are available to the spiritual man or woman. They are there; they have but to be used. When you get to the ninth sense and it is employed, you then can quickly begin to use all three senses of touch.

Fourth: The sense of the *inner spiritual touch* is a spiritual sense that allows man or woman to truly touch inside the form of the real to give assistance to or to help fill a spiritual need. Already in your time, there

Sensing: Physical and Spiritual

are those who are beginning to use this spiritual sense called the inner spiritual touch.

Fifth: The *outer spiritual touch* gives man of the spirit a third dimension that allows him to go beyond the reach of his extended arm and fingertips. Man now sends rockets to the moon or planets beyond the moon and, with mechanical means, examines the surface of the planets. I speak of a far more refined method for the spiritual man to extend his touch to a new dimension called the outer spiritual touch.

All of these senses will be dealt with under a separate study called *The Thirteen Senses of Man*. It will be a little, spiritual publication that will be printed by New World Publishers. That matter will be prepared later.

Sixth: The next is *physical sight*, and that is the one employed by man now. As his eyes receive light waves of various lengths, they are translated into objects as well as color.

Seventh: This sense is called *second sight*, which allows man to pick up light waves on either side of the scale he now employs when he wishes to see. He will be able to close his eyes, shut out the normal waves, and see with a new and wider range than will be employed by the physical man or woman.

Eighth: The *sense of refreshment* you have divided into two senses called smell and taste. They are really two parts of a single sense given to man for him to enjoy the things he uses to sustain his physical form. It was meant for mankind to enjoy his time of refreshment. He has now created many new problems for himself over this very same matter.

Ninth: With the *sense of knowing*, we now move into the range of the five powerful senses that were for the spiritual man whom I created and put in the garden. This sense allows man of the spirit to share with me in knowing, and thus, he is able to employ many new procedures to improve the life of men about him. It is this sense that the spiritual man employs to help bring things of the spirit into manifest form. This is a sense of great power.

Tenth: The *sense of being* is able to give form to the things of your sense of knowing. It is this sense that allows man to clearly sense the values of the matters of his knowing.

Eleventh: The *sense of life*, for the spiritual, not only allows the person filled with me to understand the true values of life, but how to put life into the form of your handiwork. My Son the Christ called some forth from the dead and was even victorious over death for himself. It was this spiritual sense that he employed.

Twelfth: The *sense of spiritual love* is a vibration that enables man to do many wonderful deeds of the spirit. "It has a great many usages for man of the spirit that will assist him as he seeks to lift up his fellow men and guide them unto the light of their salvation," saith the Lord thy God.

Thirteenth: The *sense of the universal* is a sense employed by my Son the Christ. It enabled him to look from a new height and perspective as he viewed the earth and his task upon it. He saw from a new and wide range of things to come as well as things going on in other places in God's vast kingdom.

I say unto you as my children, these senses are for you, every one, and they will bring great change to your society, and the changes will be called good by both the spiritual men of my creation as well as myself.

"This lesson ends with the challenge for you to turn unto me and to begin to use all that I have for you," saith the Lord thy God.

The lesson is ended. It awaits you so it may begin again.

The Spiritual Quest

LESSON 41

SPIRITUAL CREATIVTY

Write.

Man of the spirit was given all tools necessary to build and develop the world around him. When he turned from me, he gave up the fullness of his creativity along with many other spiritual tools.

Man will quickly respond by saying, "Look at my cities, inventions, the arts, and you can see that man is still very creative."

It is true that here and there a man or woman will have special creative talents and work to display them. The Spirit of my giving is in the center of every man, and as it is allowed to express itself, man's creativity is seen. Some, for moments or days, become inspired and excel in creativity for a project or for a season. There are some who are caught up by the inspiration and spend their lives with great creative talent. I say unto you as the true spirit of man is allowed to express itself, his creativity can be seen. Those moments that man calls inspiration are but spiritual path crossings, for man wanders from side to side and will cross the path of the spiritual reality of the Creator. I am the Lord God and

The Spiritual Quest

Creator of all the universe. I am spirit, and it is my Spirit that is the source of true creativity. Man of the spirit has the original source of creativity at his spiritual fingertips. Let me help you to understand more clearly the true meaning of spiritual creativity and how it is unlike shadow man's creativity and, finally, how you may become truly creative.

If we were to use the illustrations of creativity usually given by men, we could quickly see what he calls creativity is not creativity at all. He looks at a city, and he says, "See all that man has created." I would say unto you, "What you see is not creativity." There is much building and construction before you, but very little creativity. The architect who designs the building has studied all existing plans, and he designs according to many existing patterns.

Most of what you see is but a system of copies of the works of others. In reality, there is very little creativity to it at all. Even in art, many students study a copy of an accepted system. The work or art may be original and yet not truly creative. In the field of inventions, we see more creativity, but still for the most part, we seek to improve upon an accepted system. For example, someone invented the car for land travel. Man has now spent years changing and improving the original invention. He has not, however, come up with a new system of land travel. Man quickly responds, "If he invented a new system that did not use oil and gasoline, we would ruin the economy."

Let me go back a few years, and we find man saying, "If we allow this invention of the automobile, it will ruin the buggy-and-horse business." The new can always replace the old, and you will find the new will create more jobs and opportunities than were found in the old.

Spiritual Creativity

Greed greatly impedes the progress of man, and much creativity could come forward if greed were set aside. "Greed is of man of the flesh, and creativity is of the spirit," saith the Lord God, who made the heavens and the earth.

Now do you understand that when you look at the skyline of a great city, you are looking at the limitation of a limited man who will not allow his true spirit to rule his life? Thus, his creativity is but a series of spotted moments, while in my original plan for him, man of the spirit was to walk in creativity moment by moment. It was not a gift for a select few, but is for every man and woman whom I call my child.

The true creativity of the spirit man is not a brief moment, but every moment that he has need to create as he walks in the spirit. The spirit man or woman does not "copy with changes" from the work of other men, but, in fact, goes to the source where all creativity may be found, and then the work is new, original, and truly creative. The world then acclaims that they have found another genius, while in reality, the spirit spark of that one was allowed to express itself. That spark is inside every man and woman who walk upon the earth. For everyone, in reality, is a child of the Lord God, and I have made each creative in his nature.

When man turned from me, he lost his true contact with the creative reality of my Spirit. I did not take away man's creativity, for my love for him is as it was in the beginning. I do not ever take away from man my gifts or the offer of them. Man turns away from me and gives control to the body while the spirit holds the gift of creativity. Let me now speak of the steps necessary for man to regain his place of true creativity.

First: As long as the shadow of the real is in control, the real cannot operate. Man must then hear the truth that he can return to his true creative self.

Second: Men must accept the truth of my Word and take it unto themselves for what it is. This is, in fact, the turning back unto me that must be the decision and act of every man. When the real of man, his spirit, is given charge, then the blindness of the earthly is gone, and the true light that is of my Spirit is before him.

Third: Now the spirit man can once again grow and learn for he can now employ all the tools of the spirit that are for his using. His senses of knowing and of being are great helps for him in his spiritual growth.

Fourth: His walk with me must now be constant. "He cannot be with me for a day and then dart off on his own path again and then return for the blackness of his new path will make it more difficult for him to find the true path of my Spirit," saith the Lord thy God.

Fifth: He must find the proper task for his spirit in which to put his newfound creativity to work. The task will be plainly before him as he walks in the light.

Sixth: He will then call upon the source where all creativity may be found, for all of his needs shall be met with the fullness of my Spirit.

Seventh: His creative work will be called good, and he will give thanks and be in the thankful spirit of praise, for his creativity has been used to help others around him. There is no value to build or to create on the shadow of the real for it will soon be torn down to make room for more of the same.

Spiritual Creativity

Let your creativity be of the spirit, and you will be truly creative, and your work will be lasting, and you will be a blessing to all men. I am the Creator, and thus, it is I, the Father of all, who stand before you ready.

The lesson ends calling you to become the creative spirit you were made to be.

The Spiritual Quest

LESSON 42

SPIRITUAL GROWING

This lesson is one of the most important, for by it, many of the other lessons can be applied. Let it be clearly understood that man cannot straddle the two paths and keep one hand on the matters of the spirit while the other is found to grasp the matters of the earthly shadow. Man cannot deal with the real and the unreal at the same time. I have said it in my Word that man cannot serve two masters, and my Word was a truth then, and truth is eternal. All too many men and women have taken this truth lightly, and thus, they end in chaos and tragedy and find they have no spiritual life at all.

To you who read these words, I say you must choose this day the path that you are to follow. If it is the path of the Spirit, then come unto me, and look not back upon the old for it is gone from you as you walk in the spirit. If you choose to remain in the path of the world, then it is your choice, for I have made you free. But know this: The gifts that are for you will not be yours to hold or employ, and there will be no need to read further the words of this lesson for they are not for the child who chooses to walk in his own path. Again I say you will hold to one and turn from the other, for you cannot have them both in your grasp. Which will it be? You must choose now for there are no more steps for us to take unless we walk the path of my creation – the house of eternity!

Good. Now as spirit children, let us talk of the matters of your spirits' growing.

First: The first step must be taken before we could discuss any other matters. Man or woman must choose to walk the path of the Creator God.

Second: You must now know the pace of your growth is dependent upon you. All that I have for you is ready, but only as you know in the spirit can you pick up and use your spiritual tools.

Third: Allow my Word and the instruction of other spirit-filled people around you to help you as you begin. You now walk in the path of light, and there is no darkness in it at all, and so your spirit, which is of me, will assist you in each step you take.

Fourth: You will always be full when you walk in the spirit; only the capacity is changed in your growth. Hear the words of this parable well. Two women went to the well to get water. One looked the house over and found a sewing thimble, and since it was all she could find, it was her container. She arrived at the well and found there was an ever-flowing supply of water. She dipped in and filled her thimble and returned to her house. There was little she could do with the water she had, but what she had was very useful indeed. She poured it upon a plant in the window, and it gave a much needed refreshment to the dry plant. She went with her container empty, and she returned with her container filled. She was only limited in the good she could do by the size of the container she took to the well.

The second woman looked and also found a thimble, but said, "Though it is a container, it is far too small for the task before me." She continued her search, and she found an old milk pail that had not been used in some time. She took the pail to the well, and with the abundance of water, she washed the outside and the inside of the pail until it was clean. Then she filled the pail full and returned to her household. She had enough to do all the tasks before her, and there was even some left to give refreshment to her and those of her household. Both women had their containers filled. It was the size of the container that determined the amount they could accomplish when they returned to their homes.

Fifth: You must clearly see the tasks that are before you and determine that you will do to completion those same tasks. There is no value in the spiritual tools if they are unused or used very little.

The using of what you have where you are helps in the growth of your capacity. Remember, in the spirit, the container will always be filled full. It is being filled so the next step may be employed.

Sixth: It is in using that the value of the spiritual tools is found. To fill a container, but to do nothing more with it after filling is to truly waste what you have, and even what you have will turn sour and will not be usable at all. Of all that is received, it is the emptying, not the filling, that is of full value. "I do not want part of what you are," saith the Lord God. "I want all that you are, for only by your giving all am I able to give you all that I have for you." Giving all of the spirit does not mean you are to have nothing for that would mean that I do not fill the empty container, and that is just not the truth of my giving. My giving is ever flowing, and so once empty, I can do nothing but fill again.

Seventh: The container changes its capacity with use. This is a spiritual truth and may not be acceptable to the men of the shadow, but nevertheless, it is the truth. With every using, there is growth, and with every growth, there is a filling, and every filling will be full. Then as you walk in the light, you will see the greater task before you. The cycle is completed, and the growth continues. The pace of the growth is yours. "Know this final word: You must give thanks for the spirit flow of giving, for in giving thanks, you keep your spiritual direction ever upon the Giver of all there is," thus saith the Lord thy God. The lesson ends, and the ever flowing of my Spirit is before you. Come and take refreshment of my Spirit.

The Spiritual Quest

Series Seven

VII

The Spiritual Quest

LESSON 43

SPIRITUAL INSTRUCTION

Write. I speak to you now about the matter that is important to all of my spiritual children.

"Through this, my son and scribe, I have sent words to help all men and women to come unto me. This call was a spirit-to-spirit call, and the limitation in these words and lessons have been in the scribe and not in my Spirit," saith the Lord God. I would speak to you everyone daily. I would speak clearly and fully as to your responsibilities, this and every day.

I have many messengers, but you will find that there is only one message. I would not instruct you, my children, in one direction through one servant and in another direction through another servant. I tell you now signs that will speak to your spirits. If you follow these clearly, you will not be led astray.

There is truth in my Word, and none of my words are spoken outside truth. If in your spirit you have a knowing it is not truth, then it is not of me. The key words here are *truth*, *spirit*, and *knowing*.

The Spiritual Quest

First: You cannot examine my words with your minds and separate truth and error. It is a matter for the spirit, for the spirit is real, and truth is real, and the real will always know the real.

Second: The word here for the knowing of the spirit is a gift to the real spiritual man and will not abide in the man of the flesh no matter how bright a mind he may have. Not even the gathering of the world's brightest 100 minds could come to know or understand even the simplest instruction of God's Spirit unto your true spirit.

Third: The two are worlds apart and cannot be brought together by intellect. My Word, the Scripture, is real and truth, and you must allow your spirit to gather for you what is needed. The words that I have given through this, my son, are truth, and they will find full support in my Scripture. If the words of the scribe cannot be so supported, they are not for you to follow. I have said it is old treasure in new canvas. The value is in the treasure and not in the canvas that holds it or brings it unto you.

Fourth: If the words given by one who claims to have received of me do not direct all men unto the Creator God of all things, then the words are as false as the one who brings them forth. When men are directed unto other men, ideas, philosophies, or any other forms that do not bring the child unto the Creator God, then they are not of my Spirit.

Fifth: Prove the words by time and event, for when I say it shall come to pass or it shall be as I have said it, you may know it by the truth that the event bears upon it. I have made man free to choose, and so there are matters that can go either way depending upon the choice of the child of my love, called the form man. I will speak to these matters in such a way you will know what is the proper choice made in the spirit, and the

Spiritual Instruction

outcome will be as the spirit directs.

Sixth: Ponder the words within, and allow the Spirit of me that is within you to examine the matter you have brought unto it. The Spirit within will not direct you wrongly for I am spirit and there is no error within me at all.

Seventh: Ask in the spirit directly as to the validity of what someone has given you, and in spirit, I will answer. Act upon the words that have come to you as instruction and have been confirmed by your spirit, and you will see quickly the results that come forth are as my instructions have said.

I have given you in this lesson seven tests that you may use and that will be a guide to you. The results will bring a joy of the spirit to you as you study and as you then allow the Spirit of God to direct your paths.

The Spirit of God is within every child at the very center of his or her being. When you are once again spirit of my Spirit, and the form, or the body, follows the instructions of the spirit, then I will be able to direct you from within. The purpose of these lessons is not for you to become dependent upon these lessons or upon the one who brings them unto you. They are intended so that you come to a place where you receive your instruction from the Spirit of God and will then only use these lessons to help direct another child unto me.

Let your spirit know my love, and you will begin to give forth my love unto others. The fruit that you have in spirit will be evidence of how well you have learned from these lessons. When a step is taken, you then are to be up higher where the view is clearer. The step remains behind for others who shall follow after you in their search for the truth that is of me. If, when a step was finished by you, it was taken up and put away, then what would there be for those to follow? What would they stand upon to prepare themselves for the next step?

The lesson ends. May you be guided by the love of the Lord God Creator.

LESSON 44

LIGHT AND DARKNESS: SHADES OF THE SPIRIT

I would tell you now clearly that all that is of God is good, and there is light in all that is of God. There is no darkness in my creation at all. All of the spirit is light. One ray of light is light. All of the rays that make up my splendor, called light, are not called by any other name than light.

Night and day are both filled with light, for all that I have made is light and cannot be of anything else. Man of the flesh says, "Why then can I see in the day and not so well at night?" The problem is that man of the flesh uses his physical senses only to determine the scope of any matter. He then uses mental reason and does not employ any of the wide range of spiritual tools that would allow him to broaden his scope beyond his present range of sensing. There are creatures of the earth that use night as the period of their activity. The sensors of their eyes are tuned to see clearly at night while the light called day would be for them as night is for you. Your ease of seeing in the day is their hour of difficulty. Let me clearly say then all that is of God is light, be it called the light of day or the light of night.

Darkness, in its true sense, is a creation of the shadow, or the form, man. He thinks he is able to hide if he uses the blanket of night to hide his deeds from other men. Darkness is man-made and is an illusion, as is the shadow that created it. The word *darkness*, then, is a term denoting that which is other than light and spirit.

When man of the flesh is in control, he walks in darkness, and there is no light to lighten his path. It is of his choosing, for there is light waiting for him once he grows tired and weary of the path that he now follows.

Let me speak to you of a parable of four children.

The first child in trying to hide stands very still in the center of her yard and places her hands over her eyes. She now is in darkness, and since she cannot see, she believes she is hidden. The father comes home and sees her standing in the yard and says, "Where is my little girl, oh I wonder where she can be?" She takes her hands off her eyes and runs to her father and says, "Here I am!" And so the darkness has ended, and she is once again with her father. Learn from this child. Her father truly knew where she was for what was darkness to her was a full light to her father.

The second little child is in the yard playing, and he sees his father coming, and he runs and lies on the ground behind a bush and is totally out of his father's sight. His father comes home and says; "I wonder where my son is, oh where could he be?" For the father saw the son in the yard long before the son knew of the approach of his father. Thus to the father's knowing, his son was not hidden at all. The father had seen

Light and Darkness: Shades of the Spirit

all that the son had done, but in love played the fun game with his child.

The heavenly Father is all knowing and has no limitation at all. There is no place where his child can truly hide and be beyond his Father's knowing.

Learn from the child and run to the Father, for you are clearly in his knowing.

In the third yard, there are two children playing, and they are unaware of any approaching danger. A big dog approaches the yard, and the mother and father come out on the porch, and the dog turns and goes another way seeing the father and mother protectors. The children finish their play and come inside safely unaware of the watchful care of the father and mother. Learn from this lesson of the children and know that your father-mother God is watching over you.

God is light, and there is no darkness in him at all. Therefore, man cannot hide by any means from the father-mother God who sees, knows, and protects the children of his great love.

Do you see that the form calls light "darkness" and then believes he or she is not seen and goes on and does the deed under the cover of darkness where there is no cover at all and, in fact, no darkness as well?

Man may hide from man like one shadow may hide from another, but both are unreal, and so they play their games of non-reality. God is real. God is love. God is light.

Man says there are shades of the spirit. God says there is only light.

Man says, "I can hide in darkness and do my deeds of sin." God says there is no darkness, and therefore, there is no hiding place for man to go. Man calls his deeds of darkness sin. God says he does not even look upon the unreal acts of the shadow man.

Man runs to hide from God. God stands at the center of his hiding place and says in love, "Come unto me."

The lesson ends with no place for man to go but unto God the Creator.

LESSON 45

PHYSICAL AND SPIRITUAL SIN

Write, for you have had a day of rest and refreshment, and I have much to share with you this day.

You do rightly not to respond to the pressures or rushes of men around you. They were not, in truth, trying to rush you along, but I used it to see that you would not be anxious and would wait upon me. I will direct your path, and the words I now give you are for the good of all men.

The spirit man is the real man, and he is eternal. The physical man I call the form or shadow man is the manifestation of the real and is temporal. "On my part, there are no sins of the temporal man that will keep him from me," saith the Lord God. Every possible sin of the temporal man is forgivable. All he must do is let go of all that he is and turn unto me and become all I have planned for him to be. When the shadow of the real man turns unto me, his back is toward all of his past sins, and I have said unto you clearly that I never look upon them. They are gone forever; they are as if they had never been! My grace is sufficient for all things. This is my truth and it is eternal in nature. There is no eternal quality in the temporal form of man, and therefore, none of his deeds, both good or bad by his terms, have any eternal quality to them all. Notice I have said *his deeds, both good or bad.*

There is nothing eternal in nature in the accomplishments of the physical man, who is not directed by the spirit of the Creator within him. Likewise, there is nothing eternal in the nature of the failure of the physical man, who is directed by his own rebellious nature.

Since man of the flesh is only a manifestation of the real and it is not the real, then all of his "sins" are but manifestations from the unreal man of the flesh. Sin that has no reality to it is not even looked upon by the Creator God.

I hold the spirit of every man, which is the real, for I am spirit, and I am all there is. There is nothing outside the reality of the living God. The shadow man can, with his hands, make many images on the wall, and they will move as he makes them move. But image does not make a thing real. Movement does not make a thing real. Manifestation does not make a thing real. Only that which is real in the beginning has the ability to make reality for reality cannot come from any other creative source but reality.

God is real. God is spirit. Spirit is real. Spirit man is real, for he is the result of a creative act of the creative, real God. Spirit man is real, and therefore, his direct rebellion is to turn from the real, which he is, and to give the control over to the shadow of the real, called the earthly or fleshly man.

If spirit-to-spirit the Lord God is fully and finally rejected, then that spirit has separated himself from the Creator, and if the separation be full and final, then that spirit will exist no longer, and the shadow of that same spirit will exist no longer as well. That is the only true death that can occur and is on the level of the spirit. Therefore, there are two kinds of spirit rebellion. In one, the spirit turns and gives control to the form. That kind of rebellion can be won back by my love and, therefore, is not unpardonable. It is very difficult for the form to try and operate his control without the true direction of the spirit, and that is why the earthly man has so many problems that he has caused for himself. I say he brings upon himself all that is of a difficulty to him. The spirit who does not give control over to the form, but spirit-to-spirit rebels against me, that spirit will speak, and because spirit is real, the words of the rebellious spirit will be a reality for that one. The spirit that says fully and finally, "I want to be alone; I want to be separate," that spirit may say it is final, and so it will be.

Therefore, the two kinds of sin that I spoke of so far are both spiritual in nature. One is forgivable, and the other, by its rebellious nature, is unforgivable. One spirit has turned from me and has given control to the form man, whom you know as the earthly man. The other spirit has faced me and spirit-to-spirit has made a separation from the Creator God, and such a separation is full and final, for only spirit is real, and only spirit can make such a separation. The sin against the Holy Spirit is a spirit-to-spirit sin and not a sin of the flesh, or shadow, against the spirit. The two are not in the same realm, and therefore, the one (the flesh) cannot sin against the other (the spirit).

When the spirit of one has made the separation, it soon becomes evident in the form for it, too, is separated because of the act of the spirit. Do you see it is not the form or the flesh that first makes the separation, but the spirit first becomes separated, and then the form of the real must follow what the real has done?

Do not blame the flesh man for the rebellion. It was his spirit that rebelled, and the form followed for the shadow must always follow the path of the real, which I call spirit of my Spirit.

There is now a third kind of sin that is the most familiar to the fleshly man, for it is indeed the sins of the form, or the shadow, man. These sins can be as varied as all the minds and bodies in their rebellious state can conjure up.

Sin is like being blindfolded tightly until no light can come in at all and then being handed a weapon of rapid fire, but before you are told to start shooting, you are spun around at great speed. When all this is done, you are then told to hit the target with no further directions.

How many rounds of firing do you believe would be necessary for you to hit the target? How many more would be required for you to hit the center of the target? How many more would it require for you to hit the target with regularity? Man of the flesh would say it probably would take thousands of misses to get one hit, and thousands more to get any kind of regularity to your aim. In this simple parable, the target is spiritual accomplishment, and the center of the target would be a full and proper spiritual accomplishment for the one firing the weapon. The weapon would contain all the activity of the fleshly form, and bullets would be the effort given with the force behind it to reach the goal. The misses would be the sins of the form man that had enough energy expended to accomplish a given goal, but with no sight, no direction, and no perspective. When man of the form allows the control to be

Physical and Spiritual Sin

given back once again to the true and the real, which I call spirit of my Spirit, the spinning is gone, and the target is in clear view. The blindfold is removed, and you are directed by the Giver of all in this analogy. It is the Spirit of God who clears the spinning and who gives light and directs the efforts of the child of the spirit.

"What about the sins of the fleshly man?" says the child who is seeking.

I say unto you, "What about them?" Turn from them, and for you they are gone. For me, the Lord God, they are gone as well. Do not look back for I do not look upon them ever again.

I have spoken to you of three forms of sin, for they are all called by the same name. Sins of the shadow are sin. The sins of the spirit who turns from me are sin. The sin of the spirit who rejects me is sin indeed! What do I call them? I call them sin!

Who forgives the sins of the flesh? Who turns his back upon them?

Shadows cast by the shadow man are still shadows. The spirit that severs the spirit ties is severed indeed. I do not then single out one sin from another.

Anything done by the unreal is, in fact, unreal, and there are not degrees of unreality. Anything done by the spirit is, in fact, real since the spirit is real, and yet there are not degrees to this reality: The spirit that turns from me has turned. Anything done by the spirit in full and final separation is real, and the separation is full and final, and there is no degree to this reality as well.

The lesson ends. What now shall become of your sins? What now shall become of you, the sinner?

Let your spirit return unto me, and we shall be one once again, and your sins will be no more.

LESSON 46

THE SPIRITUAL OFFERING AND HEAVENLY CAUTIONS

The only true offering that man can give to the Father is the gift of himself, and it must be the full gift of self. If all that you are is given over to God, then all that you have will be given as well. I speak in spirit terms and not physical. I do not require you to dispose of any of your earthly possessions. I do require you to let go of your hold on all of your earthly possessions. Those who walk in the spirit have all that is of God waiting for them and for their full use. Do the will of the Father, and the spiritual offering is complete.

In my Old Testament Word, as it is called, did I not have one of my sons place his son on the altar to take his life? Both were my sons, and I would not have one take the life of the other. Their willingness to give all was all that was required. Then the lamb was found in the thicket, and the sacrifice was made. My Son the Christ is the lamb caught in the nearby thicket and was sacrificed by his willingness, not by the commands of the shadows around him. He could have called light from the heavens, and light will always make the shadow vanish from the face of the earth. In another lesson, I will speak more on this matter. Christ gave freely in order that you may have an example of all giving and, thus, be able to give your all.

The cautions I have for you go along with every spiritual offering. Do not offer a part of yourself and call it your all, for I am all knowing, and I will know how much you hold in reserve from me. To hold from me is to not have truly given at all. Thinking that you have anything you can give other than yourself and that the Lord God will accept and be pleased is a folly of man.

Things given may be accepted by men, and yet I have given no acceptance to them at all. Give first all that you are, and then anything of substance you give, even one penny, will be of value to my work for my work is spirit and requires you first before the offering of substance. I would rather give you much substance than receive any substance from you and not have all of the real gift, the gift of yourself. You are truly spirit, and it is spirit that can receive of the spirit.

Do not be deceived by many of the works in the present church, for much of it is man-made and not of my Spirit. Do not concern yourself with these works for I tell you now a truth. When you have given me your all, there is nothing the hands of man can do to you for you are spirit and spirit is eternal. If they destroy the body, they have only stamped their feet upon the shadow, and the real is unchanged and undamaged by their stamping. "Do not fear," is the caution that goes with this truth for men cannot deal with the spirit and that is what you are, my sons and daughters in me.

Offer me the tools of your body. Your hands will move with swiftness to the need that is for them. Your feet will go according to my call, and you will find that my Spirit will not take you any place that will not be found for your good. All that you are in the form, now under control of the spirit, will move by the pleasure of the Lord God and Creator.

The caution is that you move under the direction of the Spirit and not by the whimsical call of men, for they will get a thought which is of the mind, and then they will share it with you and call it spirit. "You are to come here and go there," they will say. You will answer, "No, I go where I am led of the Father," and quickly you will find that they will adjust their plans accordingly.

Remember that what you do and where you go are a spiritual offering unto me, and therefore, you will do as the spirit directs and not move under the direction of men of the flesh.

When you pause daily to be refreshed of me and we, spirit to spirit, have communion one with another, know this is a spiritual offering unto me and one of great value. It is valuable to me for at that time, I am able to give unto you your spiritual refreshment, rest, and instruction so that you are better able to share with all of my children.

I would have you hear this spiritual caution of me: Do not allow the matters that are around you to take away this time from you. We must be together every day, for our walk is for the good of all men. Protect our moments together like you count them as precious as they really are.

You must not be afraid of giving all that you have of yourself to others at any time, providing their need is truly and clearly brought before your spirit. You will know in spirit when it is proper to give, so give, for it is a blessing to me when you empty yourself before others. It is the emptying of yourself that makes it possible for more filling to come forth from me. I give you the caution on this matter as well. The caution is twofold, and either of the two could hurt the work that is before you.

When it is needed for you to give your all, do it, for I will fill you, and you will know no loss within you. The second caution on this matter is you are not to empty any of my word and truth if it will be rejected by the child, or the children, with whom you are about to share. It would surely be a waste for it would be like pouring precious oil upon the ground. It would be quickly absorbed by the ground and gone, and there would be no change in the earth that would be of any eternal value.

This lesson is for every child who wishes to teach and raise others up in the spirit. I will guide you, everyone, if you will give yourself over to me. That is the offering of which I speak.

You are the gift that is pleasing unto me when it is brought before me.

The lesson ends. The giving begins.

LESSON 47

VALUES BOTH EARTHLY AND SPIRITUAL

This lesson is given so man of the flesh will clearly understand with his mind and know that he has nothing. This lesson is given so man of the spirit will understand with his spiritual knowing and know that he has everything.

The man of the earth may have much wealth and yet truly have nothing because of his value placed upon his wealth, while the man of the spirit may have much wealth and counts it as nothing, but uses his wealth for the glory of God. The spirit man, therefore, has much wealth of the earth that is counted as nothing by him, but is used much for his Lord God. Since the spirit man is a spirit, he has much wealth of the spirit that is counted as everything, and his values are in proper order.

If his physical wealth, to him, is counted as nothing, then "things" are at value zero at this point in relation to true value. He now may have everything that is counted as real to the spirit, and then his true value is counted as great.

Value is found in that which has some quality of eternal value in it. The key word here is *eternal*. That which is eternal is of value, and that which is temporal is of no value in relationship to the eternal.

The earthly and the temporal are one and the same. There is no eternal value in anything earthly. The spiritual is eternal; they are one and the same. There is all eternal value in anything spiritual.

Now what of man's employment of this great truth?

First, let every man know that once he lets the spirit control, any need of a spiritual nature is his for the asking. Now hear me again very clearly: Any need of a physical nature is for the asking of the spiritual man for his need will always be used for a spiritual purpose.

There is no value for the spiritual man to take the vow of poverty. It would be better for him to take the vow of great riches for riches in the hands of the spirit man will always find a good and proper place for their using.

Any wealth in the hands of the man of the flesh will be wasted, or at least spent on that which is temporal in nature, and, thus in a final word, wasted indeed.

There are men who seek to become spiritual, and thus, they take the vow of poverty to assist them in their quest. I say unto you now so you may clearly know, "Turn unto me, and the first thing you will drop is your control of your life by the hands of the form." Let your spirit, which is real, control, and you will not go in any direction contrary to the truth and the right path for you. Next, drop your vow of poverty, and ask God to supply your every need while you live your life in the spirit in the service of the Lord God, the Creator and Giver of every perfect gift. I tell you if the wealth of all the world, now at the very hour of this reading, were given unto you in one large pile, it would be as one grain of sand compared to all the sands of all the beaches of all the seas of all the worlds if we were to compare the wealth of the storehouse of God with the wealth of man.

The wealth of man is for the man of the flesh for it is his illusion and it is made by him.

The wealth of God is for the spirit man of God, for it is God's reality, and it is made by God for the use of the spirit man. Drop the very word *poverty* for it is man-made and not God-made. I, your Father God, have used the word, but only to have you rid yourself of the word and all that it implies.

If the kind king of a great land had riches untold, and his son who was once lost, but now is found, had a need, would not the king supply? Would not the kind king say to his son, "All that is mine is yours as well."

If the earthly king of kindness knows how to give to his son whom he loves, how much more will I give unto you if you but ask me? You must indeed first know you are my son before you will ask, not that I am not willing to give, but it is yours for the asking, and I will not force upon you that which you have not requested as my son. Whenever he is told to go, he knows that whatever need he has, as my son, will be supplied.

Do not change your plans; just begin so the supply may come for if you wait for the supply to come first before you begin, there will be no supply as well as no beginning. There are many men of the shadow who say unto other men, "When I get all things right, I'll come to God." They cannot, they do not, and so they never come unto me.

When one child says, "I come unto the Lord and Creator God as I am, with all my problems and sins before me," the moment he takes that first step unto me, the problems and sins are gone. Know the order with which things of the spirit are done. The flesh works differently and is not the real, but only the shadow of the real. The spirit is real, and I am real for I am spirit. The need of the spirit man is expressed in his doing the requests of the spirit, and thus, the supply is able to come. This is a very important lesson for all my children of the spirit to learn. You must know the law of spiritual manifestation and this lesson which activates it. Let these words speak to the spirits of all men. The lesson ends with a value to your spirit.

LESSON 48

THE GLORY OF THE TRUE NEW AGE

Write.

The true *new age* is one where man will turn more and more back unto the Lord God his Creator, and then the plans that I have for the spiritual man will be able to develop for the good of all men.

When man of the spirit is in charge of the life and the form is then being directed by the spirit, the glory will be properly directed to the Spirit of God.

The true new age will be marked by the increase of love of one for another. As the spirit man controls, he becomes a giver of love, and as the love vibration increases, more and more children will be drawn unto me.

The true new age will be marked by the new power of the spirit, a power to accomplish for the good of all men. You will see the results of spiritual healing, and there will be many signs the world over that the people of the spirit are growing in numbers and power.

The true new age will find man calling those around him "brothers" and "sisters," and there will be a new unity between the races of men, for the spirit man knows that all men in the spirit are brothers, one with another. The spirit movement will be one of true praise and worship. Men will step forward boldly and declare the truth of my Word to all men, and because it will be the truth, the power of the Spirit will support the effort of those who do so proclaim my truth.

There will be new value placed upon the true temple of the Lord God, and the spirit children will take proper care of their manifested forms.

The true new age will be one marked by true peace, which comes from the harmony of spirit love and spirit joy. The peace of which I speak will be found from within each man and woman of peace. It will not come from the organizations and structures now in control, but will come forward from the laymen from every walk of life and from every nation.

This land, the United States of America, will be the light center of the world, and this light will go out to all parts of the world. I am the Lord thy God, and I am light, and it is the radiance of my Spirit that shall go forth to every corner of darkness of the earth.

I have made man free, and he may choose to follow the direction of his spirit, or he may follow the dictates of the shadow form. There is life in the true new age that is now bursting on the scene, and this life will quicken the spirits of men who are open and receptive to my Spirit.

You will see, at the very same time, the results of the spirit rejection. Men of the flesh will move from one calamity unto another, and with every move that is made, they will find they have only compounded their failure. This, too, will be a sign of victory, and God will be glorified, for

The Glory of the True New Age

out of their failure, many will be presented the truth of the Spirit, and as they return unto me, their success will be even greater than the failures they have just experienced. Even in failure, God may be glorified and praised, and the brother or sister having experienced the failure will know even more – the joy of the return of the spirit unto the Spirit of God.

Man is coming out of darkness that was of his own making, and the light of his new life will be bright, shining as the noonday sun.

Men will lift their hands in praise, and I will supply their needs in abundance. In places where man is following the leading of my Spirit, you will see the abundance of my love manifest in many new and beautiful forms. Next to the man of the spirit, you may see men of the form standing, and his efforts will not be blessed, and his abundance will soon be gone. He will cry for rain, and the ground will be dry, and nothing will grow with any vigor. In anger, he will wave his clenched fist, only to find it will fall back upon him like a sledge of great weight.

This will be an age where the joy and the glory of the Lord will shine in the faces of the spirit children, and the agony of the flesh will be seen just as clearly in the faces of men of the form.

There will be waves of the Spirit's moving over areas of the land, and men and women will turn unto me with the very simplest of call.

The spirit children will give us great and beautiful songs of praise, and they will lift up my Son, Jesus of Nazareth the Christ, as the ideal for all men everywhere to follow. Idols will fall, and spirit men will stand in their places.

There will be a new spiritual thrust in government, and the spirit quality of a man or woman will become important in the selection of positions of high places. Man of the spirit will give the praise to the proper quarter, and thus, the ego of man will become less and less as the spirit grows. I am able to tell you of what is going to come to pass, but I have made man free, and therefore, I will not tell you how quickly you will choose to walk in the light that is before you.

I will tell you this: The longer man waits to allow his real spirit to control his shadow form, the longer the chaos will continue, and man will, for a season, know the agony that was his father's and his father's before him.

The true new age of which I speak is a spirit age, and therefore, it is real and will last as long as man does not turn his back on the Creator and give control to the form once again.

It will be a season of great joy for all the children, for they will be given a new place of importance, and they will be loved and taught to grow up in the Spirit. They will carry on the true new age in grand style, and the Lord God will be pleased and will give unto them abundantly. They will make strides in all fields and will bring to light truths that have been hidden from the men of the old age because of their self-imposed blindness.

It will be a time of great joy and caring for the aged of this land and every other land. They will be loved, and they will give great love in return. Many of them will accomplish their greatest work for they will be allowed full, new, and free expression of their spirits. They will find new purpose in living, and my Spirit will quicken their spirits, and thus, they will extend the length of their years in order to accomplish great new tasks before them. They will find new fulfillment and purpose, and they will give thanks unto the Lord their God, and I will surely bless them, every one.

There are volumes to be shared about this true new age, but it cannot begin until you who read these words allow the Spirit of the Lord thy God to direct your paths.

I will bring you unto the true light that is for every man, and I will open a door that shall give you a view of the things that are to come. The spirit man will see and hear and understand, and my words will fill his body, mind, and spirit. The man of the flesh will have ears to hear, and yet he will not hear. He will have eyes to see and will be blinded by the light of my truth.

This lesson ends with the call to all men to rise up and be led of the spirit, for the true new age is a spirit age, and it will bring glory to everyone. "I have spoken these words in truth," saith the Lord God. It is no longer just the beginning; my work of the true new age has already begun. Join ye this day unto me.

The Spiritual Quest

LESSON 49

THE FUTURE FROM THIS DAY FORTH

Write, for these words will carry truth forward until every word I speak herein will come to pass.

Man of the flesh has some memory of the past, but not a great deal. The present is ever before him, but even then he is unable to interpret most of what goes on around him. He uses only his earthly senses, and thus, he is limited indeed. As far as the future, he can only at best, by reading signs of the present, predict something of the future. A child with little knowledge can look at the rain clouds above and feel the change in the winds that blow against his face and say there will be rain sometime soon.

Man of the spirit has all of the tools of his spiritual Father, for I have given them unto him. He must only learn the proper use of each of them, and soon he will be looking at the future as clearly as the man of the flesh now looks at the present.

Man of the spirit will see things as they are and not as they seem to be. Therefore, he will base his new discoveries on truth, and his advancement will be great.

He will employ the natural laws of the spirit, and the creative laws of the universe will work with and for him, and therefore, things that are impossible for the shadow man will be a simple reality for the man of the spirit.

As the spirit child of my love becomes one with me, he will have the full power of the real at his fingertips. I will now speak in specifics so you may see these things come to pass, and you will know that these truths have come from the Creator and Lord of all. I have spoken, and so I say write.

Thus saith the Lord thy God, "I am light, and I am spirit, and so man of the spirit will find the true use of light, and thus, he will build a new form of structure from my light under the pressure of a constant." This new building material will be lighter than aluminum and stronger than steel. The cost to use this substance is nearly to a point of no cost at all. It will hold an even temperature and will resist extremes of cold and heat. It will be for the true new age like fire and the wheel were to the old.

Man will draw a new source of power from out of the air itself and at no cost to every home of the true new age. This power will run all needs of energy necessary to sustain man in comfort.

Your systems of fuel – coal, oil, and gas – will be as primitive as was the caveman's rubbing of sticks together to make fire. You will make a new fuel of water that will give you in drops power that it now takes tons of gasoline to duplicate.

Man of the spirit will learn to control the elements, and the winds and the seas will be at his command. Man of the spirit can speak the word, and in a moment, he will move mountains and make of them level plains if that is truly the need of the hour. It will make man's earth-moving machines be the outdated tools of a past age.

You will see a time when medicine will be practiced by the true spirit man, and the healings will be performed without loss of blood. Surgical tools will be looked upon with wonder in the museums of the true new age. Man will not be charged for his healing, and if he be of the spirit, he will be directed toward methods so he may be able to heal others in need.

The age of man will be extended to the length needed to do the accepted task. It will be written that men of several hundred years will be commonplace, and to die at all will be called foolish.

Men will praise their God in true spirit, and the power will be such that it will be felt on other planets of this universe. Worship will be true, and even the spoken word will cause to come to pass what was just spoken. Children will be a joy, and men will walk in harmony with one another. The hand of God will be seen in the handiwork of my children.

The wealth of today will be considered as dust when compared to the wealth of this true new age. Gold will be made as easily as plastic is in your day, and men will find many new and common uses for it. Values will be on the matters of the spirit, and so the things of the earth will be only tools to build the true new age of the spirit man.

I tell you these things so that man of the spirit may rule, and the things I have described above are but the most simple and, therefore, the most common of gifts in the hands of my children. Oh that I could see these things for the future of man, for man at this place has two futures before him. Man looks at three dimensions: his past, present, and future. I tell you that there are seven dimensions to the very first step for the spirit man and then more steps to follow. The sense of the universal, which is for every man, will open many of these new avenues of which I speak.

If man of the flesh should continue to rule, I see chaos that is so terrible that men will call for death to fall upon them, and there will be no death to step forward in answer to their call. Man of the flesh will crawl on his hands and knees in search of food and will dig the roots from the ground, even as they sprout, to seek to maintain his own life.

He will look at his skyline, and there will be no blue above his head, and there will be no sounds of birds. In the cities, tall stone and steel buildings will stand cold and empty as signs that the progress of the fleshly man was truly a road of self-destruction.

Only an honored few will have the luxury of clean water to drink – you would only use it today to wash your hands. There will be sores, sickness, and famine.

My children will live above all this, yet they will be found in it all. They will live to try and lift the man of the flesh up upon his feet once more. They will not grow weary for they will be sustained by my Spirit and I will provide for them their needs in the very center of man's chaos.

Quickly, man of the flesh cries out, "Which of these two will it be?" and I say unto him, "Man of the flesh will bring chaos, and man of the spirit will bring my true new age of glory and grandeur that only the spirit can give."

You may choose this day which of these ages will be the future for which you will labor.

The lesson ends here. Where do you choose to begin?

O Father, I wish the lessons and this work could go on.

Where have I said the work has ended? It has only begun. You have been faithful in this small task, and I have other works for you to establish.

Rest now, and take my love and joy with you, and you will be at peace.

Thus saith the Lord God of every man.

Amen and amen.

For additional copies of this book, contact your local bookstore.

You may also visit www.maxstitts.com to order this book and other materials as well as to check on future publications. For possible speaking engagements, please submit a request through the website.

Printed in the United States
23110LVS00005B/1-54